PRAISE FOR *GEMS OF GLUTEN-FREE BAKING*

I have worked as a clinical dietitian in an outpatient setting for over 25 years and have seen a huge increase in the number of clients I see with Celiac Disease.

Many of the people are shocked by their Celiac diagnosis and overwhelmed with the number of diet changes they need to make to avoid gluten-containing grains. After sampling some of the available gluten-free products in the grocery stores, people wonder what they will eat, since their first reaction is often negative. They comment that the gluten-free alternatives are dry, tasteless, lacking in nutrients and fibre and very expensive to purchase. After sampling a number of products from your cookbook, I can report that gluten-free baking can be very tasty, nutritious and easy to make.

Other Calgary dietitians and a client have remarked on your cookbook, *Gems of Gluten-Free Baking,* and been impressed with the quality of the baked products. Your cookbook includes a wide variety of well-tested recipes, offers flexibility with ingredients and has an emphasis on using whole grain, higher fibre ingredients. I find the book easy to follow and the baking tips useful.

I look forward to telling my clients about this excellent resource.

—*Jill Pearson, RD, CDE, Calgary, AB*

I have examined the book *Gems of Gluten-Free Baking* by Wendy Turnbull in detail, and have found the information very informative and well researched. The recipes and photos contained in the book give credit to the author, as I have been provided with some great-tasting samples made from these recipes.

The most significant aspect to me, as a baker for more than 40 years, is that the gluten-free products sampled much resembled the characteristics of normal yeast goods. Often gluten-free products are very dense and tend to be somewhat dry. The samples were not of that characteristic. From cinnamon buns to cookies to a delicious gingerbread with lemon sauce, all products were well appointed in taste and character.

This book will be a great service to the many persons affected by Celiac Disease and many others who make the choice for alternative baked goods.

—*Volker Baumann, Certified Master Baker, Baking and Pastry Arts Program, SAIT Polytechnic, Calgary, AB*

Recently we purchased 12 of your *Gems of Gluten-Free Baking* for our two natural health food stores as a trial. With your marketing support the copies of the book have since sold out and quite quickly. We would consider purchasing more copies in the future!

—*Frank Sarro, Purchasing Manager, Community Natural Foods Ltd., Calgary, AB*

D1122161

TESTIMONIALS

Thanks for writing such a fabulous cookbook on gluten-free baking! I'm comparatively new to the gluten-free diet and have found your recipes easy to follow and very satisfying to eat. I've had first-time luck with every recipe tried, which is a surprise to me since I have heard that gluten-free recipes can be tricky. My non gluten-free friends have eaten the Angel Food Cake and Chocolate Zucchini Cake, declaring they are "delicious." They were unable to tell they were not made with wheat flour.

Thanks for empowering me with your GEMS flour mix and recipes. The gluten-free diet doesn't seem so difficult to follow now.

—Gillian Brown, Regina, SK

On Thanksgiving Sunday I hosted my family including my 85-year-old Celiac mother. Before dinner I mentioned I had a new cookbook and was going to make some cookies after dinner. She didn't sound too excited. Following dinner her enthusiasm had increased and she ended up doing most of the preparation. She loved the Double Chocolate Drop Cookies' taste and couldn't remember when she had last eaten cookies! She took the cookies home with her—the rest of us had only one each!

Thank you for your efforts in researching and publishing the cookbook. I expect we will be baking more!

—Gail Pollock, Calgary, AB

I had the opportunity recently to review and test out the recipes in your book. Being a Celiac myself I can really appreciate the research and work you have put into your book. I like the concept of making up a flour mix that is flexible. I tried the Pecan Pie recipe and served it at Thanksgiving. Everyone thought it was great. I have lent the book to my mother who is also a Celiac. Thank you for sharing your years of experience with me and my family.

—Nicole Buchberger, Calgary, AB

Just to let you know how pleased I am with your cookbook. My husband has been on a gluten-free diet for quite some time and was extremely impressed with your muffins. Just recently I made the Buttery Dinner Rolls. I don't normally eat gluten-free food as I keep it for my husband but I did try one of the dinner rolls and couldn't believe how light and flavourful it was. I am so pleased to have found such a wonderful gluten-free cookbook.

—Maureen Stanley, Victoria, BC

Gems of Gluten-Free Baking

Gems of Gluten-Free Baking

Breads and Irresistible Treats
Everyone Can Enjoy

WENDY TURNBULL

Wendy Turnbull

whitecap

Copyright © 2008, 2010 by Wendy Turnbull

First edition published 2008 by Koiliakos Press (Calgary)

Second edition 2010 by Whitecap Books

Whitecap Books is known for its expertise in the cookbook market, and has produced some of the most innovative and familiar titles found in kitchens across North America. Visit our website at www.whitecap.ca.

Edited by Elizabeth Collins Oman
Design concept by Cheryl Peddie/Emerge Creative
Index by Karen Griffiths/Griffiths Indexing
Food photography by Todd Patterson/Ridge Rock Studios, except photo of Glazed Cinnamon
   Rolls (back cover) by Brian Harder Photography

Printed in China

Library and Archives Canada Cataloguing in Publication

Turnbull, Wendy, 1947–

   Gems of gluten-free baking : breads and irresistible treats everyone can enjoy /
Wendy Turnbull.

Includes bibliographical references and index.
ISBN 978-1-77050-018-1

   1. Gluten-free diet—Recipes. 2. Baking. I. Title.

RM237.86.T87 2010   641.5'638   C2010-900598-8

The publisher acknowledges the financial support of the Government of Canada through the Canada Book Fund (CBF) and the Province of British Columbia through the Book Publishing Tax Credit.

10 11 12 13 14   5 4 3 2 1

CONTENTS

Yeast & Quick Breads · 31
Nothing smells more enticing than the aroma of freshly baked bread.
Here is just a taste: Focaccia, Sourdough and Pumpernickel as well as Hot Cross,
Hamburger and Hot Dog Buns. For brunch, add a delicious touch with a basket
of Currant Scones, Savoury Cheese Biscuits or Irish Soda Bread.

Muffins & Tea Breads · 57
Flavours are captured in Berry Cream, Banana Nut and Lemon Poppy Seed muffins
served fresh from the oven. The scrumptious Strawberry and Rhubarb Loaf or
Spicy Pumpkin Bread will appeal even to the most finicky eater.

Cookies · 77
Everyone loves homemade cookies, especially when they're this good! From Apple 'n' Raisin
to Double Chocolate Drops, Whipped Shortbread to Coconut Macaroons, Gingersnaps
to Jam-Jams, you'll love these adaptations of time-honoured favourites.
The only hard part will be choosing which one to make first.

Squares & Bars · 105
Luscious Lemon Squares, Coconut Raspberry Bars, Apricot Squares and
Granola Bars are guaranteed winners. For a chocolate treat, indulge
in the egg- and milk-free Chocolate Fudge Brownies.

FOREWORD

It gives me great pleasure to write this foreword for *Gems of Gluten-Free Baking*.

As a gastroenterologist I see many patients with Celiac Disease. It is a very common disease in our society and we are diagnosing more and more patients with this problem. With the advent of blood tests for Celiac Disease and greater access to endoscopy, I am happy to say that we are able to diagnose most patients with this disease before significant complications occur.

Celiac Disease is an immunological reaction to gluten, which results in damage to the small intestine. The main portions of the small intestine affected by gluten are the duodenum and the jejunum. These two portions of the small intestine are critical for absorbing most of the nutrients in our daily diets. For example, iron and calcium as well as vitamins are absorbed in the duodenum and jejunum. If there is injury to the small intestine, the bowel does not absorb nutrients properly, resulting in nutrient deficiencies. These nutrient deficiencies can result in some of the complications seen in Celiac Disease, including iron deficiency (due to decreased iron absorption) and osteoporosis (due to lack of calcium and vitamin D absorption).

Once an individual is diagnosed with Celiac Disease the treatment is usually quite straightforward and requires maintaining a lifelong gluten-free diet. The main complaint I have from my patients with a recent diagnosis of Celiac Disease is that there is a limited selection of foods that they are able to eat. Gluten is found in many prepared food products, thus home baking is the best way to avoid gluten. As is well described in the introductory portions of this book, the main grains in which gluten is found are wheat, rye and barley. Thus, when cooking gluten-free one has to adapt numerous recipes to avoid using these grains. Some patients simply go the route of not ingesting any baked goods due to their poor quality, their limited availability or lack of good recipes for gluten-free baking. Clearly, those who have a diverse diet are more likely to adhere to a gluten-free diet and will derive more pleasure from eating than those who restrict themselves to a very simplistic diet to avoid eating gluten.

I hope *Gems of Gluten-Free Baking* sheds light on questions you may have about Celiac Disease and the gluten-free diet. I think books such as *Gems of Gluten-Free Baking* are excellent in providing a fantastic array of recipes for baked goods. May you enjoy many of the recipes provided in the pages of this book.

Paul L. Beck, MD, PhD, FRCPC

Dr. Paul Beck is a clinician/scientist at the University of Calgary, Division of Gastroenterology, and he specializes in treatment of patients with Inflammatory Bowel Disease and Celiac Disease. He also conducts research in the area of Celiac Disease and Inflammatory Bowel Disease.

ACKNOWLEDGEMENTS

The writing of *Gems of Gluten-Free Baking* involved more than the three and a half years it took to produce the manuscript. Many of the book's recipes evolved slowly and took time to fine-tune. I realize how fortunate I was to have the opportunity to choose whether to be a home-maker or work outside the home. *Gems of Gluten-Free Baking* would not be a reality had I chosen the latter. I am indebted to my mother for instilling her love for cooking and baking in me. With a degree in home economics she was the Martha Stewart of her day. From a very young age, when one is impressionable, I was happiest while in the kitchen—watching her and then later helping her bake. Though she died far too young her spirit has always been with me.

To my children:

Shauna—As I began this endeavour you were a source of strength and inspiration. When a sounding board was needed you were there to listen. I valued your helpful suggestions and thoughtful insights. On many occasions you would supply the word or phrase that somehow had been eluding me. I am grateful for all your assistance and I appreciate the recipes. Thank you.

Nathan—I could not have finished this project without you. Your help with the computer—in person, via the phone or by remote assistance—was invaluable. Your patience and relaxed demeanour helped reduce my stress. It's a credit to you that you could design and build the Gluten-Free Gems website. Thank you.

Tributes:

To Jacquelin Gates, a Registered Dietitian who has volunteered with the Celiac Association and counselled outpatients in Calgary for over 15 years: Thank you for your participation and enthusiasm in the writing of this book. I appreciate the time you took to review segments of *Gems of Gluten-Free Baking* and provide relevant comments.

To my good friend Jette DaSilva: Thank you for supporting my belief in the value of this book, and then encouraging me to pursue and follow it through. I am indebted to you for taking on the difficult task of editing all 128 recipes. This critical job could not have been placed in more capable hands.

To my family, relatives and friends: Thank you for being willing taste testers and pillars of support. Your comments and encouragement were always appreciated.

To my associates in the Calgary Celiac Association, Sandy Baines, Karen Renaud and Ralph Barnett: Thank you for your assistance.

To Cassidy Stockton of Bob's Red Mill: Thank you for answering my questions and supplying the sizable sample of whole grain sorghum!

Special thanks to Cheryl Peddie/Emerge Creative and Elizabeth Collins Oman. Cheryl, your creativity is evident in the brilliant design concept. Elizabeth, I relied heavily on your expertise and thorough attention to detail.

Last but not least, I acknowledge the individuals who daily face the challenges of a gluten-free diet. My hat is off to you.

INTRODUCTION

During the Calgary Celiac Association's 2006 Fall Conference, I conducted a survey on gluten-free baking. Over 100 individuals and professionals from across Alberta and Saskatchewan participated. Their responses and insights are woven throughout the pages of this book.

One of the simple pleasures of life is the enjoyment of tasty food. Who doesn't remember biting into a warm chocolate chip cookie, spreading butter and jam onto a slice of bread or sharing a birthday cake with family and friends? We often take these moments for granted until they are no longer an option. This is the case for individuals who are gluten intolerant.

As a baby in the late 1940s I became gravely ill when a wheat-based infant cereal called Pablum was introduced into my diet. Under formidable circumstances a diagnosis of Celiac Disease was finally made. My parents were told it was a childhood condition that one outgrows. After several months on a strict diet of bananas and cottage cheese my health appeared to be back to normal. Over the next few years my mother carefully introduced new foods until I was eating a normal diet. It was not until 30 years later that my Celiac Disease was formally diagnosed with a small bowel biopsy. By then it had been determined that Celiac Disease is a condition a person does not outgrow. I was instructed to adopt a gluten-free diet and make it a lifelong commitment.

At that time there were few gluten-free products available and very few cookbooks. As increasing numbers of people were diagnosed with Celiac Disease, manufacturers tried to keep pace by providing a greater selection of gluten-free products. Unfortunately baked items, particularly breads, have been and still continue to be disappointing to eat, visually unappealing, dry and crumbly. I attributed the problem to the basic flour mix used in gluten-free baking, consisting primarily of refined starch and/or white rice flour.

Having a vested and long-standing interest in improving the quality of gluten-free baking, I set out to find a suitable replacement flour. Over a period of years I became familiar with 13 whole grain gluten-free flours, one at a time. Each was tested by baking a loaf of bread. The purpose of this was to determine their individual traits. This information was used to make combinations of flours that complemented one another. The blends that resulted had many of the same properties as wheat flour. The formula that led to the GEMS flour evolved from this testing process. It requires four whole grain gluten-free flours. The first two flours must be included; the next two offer a choice based on personal preference, availability or cost.

All GEMS flour combinations yield a superb loaf of bread. Breads and other items prepared with the GEMS flour are tasty and crumble free, moist with a wheat-like texture. Individuals following a gluten-free diet comment on how good the baking is and those on a regular diet are surprised to learn the items are not prepared with wheat flour. I am delighted to pass along these delicious recipes everyone can enjoy, adapted for use with nutritious whole grain flours and suitable for any occasion. Whether a novice or an expert, I hope *Gems of Gluten-Free Baking* will be educational, as well as motivating and inspiring. So warm up the kitchen, invite in family and friends and enjoy the tasty home-baked goodies—one of life's simple pleasures.

WHAT IS CELIAC DISEASE AND DERMATITIS HERPETIFORMIS?

As far back as AD 250, a Greek physician chronicled one of our first records of Celiac. Aretaeus of Cappadocia used the Greek word *koiliakos* to describe suffering in the bowels. Over time the *k* became *c* and *oi* became *oe*. When the Greek ending *os* was dropped it gave us the word *Coeliac*.

Celiac Disease is due to an immunological response to gluten, which is a component of wheat, rye, barley and a variety of other grains. This immunological response results in injury to the small intestine. The damage to the small intestine can cause malabsorption (the inability of your body to digest and absorb food). This damage and malabsorption can cause diarrhea, malnutrition and nutrient deficiencies. The illness can affect people of all ages. It is most common in Caucasian populations but has been reported worldwide. Recently it has been recognized that Celiac Disease is much more common than we thought. Depending on the study and patient population, it can affect 1 in 500 or up to 1 in 150. Often there is a delay in diagnosis or patients are never diagnosed since many people have few or no significant symptoms yet still develop nutritional deficiencies and other problems such as osteoporosis and anemia.

There is a clear genetic component to Celiac Disease with almost all patients having a specific genetic background or tissue type. If one identical twin has Celiac Disease the other twin will have a greater than 70 percent chance of having or developing it. The disease runs in families with 10 to 20 percent of patients having a first- or second-degree relative affected. If you have Celiac Disease then there is an increased chance that your parents, siblings and children have or will develop the disease.

The only treatment available for Celiac Disease is to completely avoid ingestion of gluten. Most respond quickly and completely to a gluten-free diet. Untreated it can cause numerous problems primarily related to malabsorption. Although most patients present with mild to moderate symptoms, some can present with severe symptoms that can be life threatening. Celiac Disease is considered to be an autoimmune disease that is triggered by gluten. As with other autoimmune diseases, having this disease means an increased risk of having diabetes, arthritis, thyroid-related disorders and skin rashes. It also increases one's risk for developing some specific types of cancer, including small bowel cancer and less commonly colon cancer. Studies have shown that after being on a gluten-free diet for five or more years your risk of these cancers equals that of the general population.

The common way to diagnose Celiac Disease is by doing an upper endoscopy, which involves putting a tube into the mouth and advancing it through the stomach and into the small bowel where biopsies are taken. Blood tests are also available to screen for the disease. These are generally good tests, but sometimes the tests can be negative when indeed the patient has the disease and sometimes they can be positive when the person does not have it. This is why the endoscopic biopsy approach is so important. Following treatment with a gluten-free diet allows the small intestine returns to normal, but this can take variable amounts of time.

Dermatitis Herpetiformis is a chronic skin disorder that is characterized by a rash that often has small blister-like lesions and is usually intensely itchy. Although it can occur on any part of the skin, it is more common on elbows, knees, lower back and buttocks. Some studies suggest that most, if not all, patients with Dermatitis Herpetiformis have Celiac Disease. Both conditions usually respond well to a gluten-free diet. Celiac Disease is usually associated with Dermatitis Herpetiformis, as both are autoimmune disorders triggered by the ingestion of gluten. Like Celiac Disease, control for Dermatitis Herpetiformis necessitates following a gluten-free diet. At present there is no cure for either Celiac Disease or Dermatitis Herpetiformis, and thus these individuals must be on a lifelong gluten-free diet.

CHALLENGES OF THE GLUTEN-FREE DIET

In order to maintain optimum health, Canada's Food Guide recommends individuals eat a balanced diet from the four food groups: vegetables and fruits; grain products; milk and alternatives; and meat and alternatives. The suggested number of servings per day in each category is based on the nutrient requirements for each gender and age. Most Canadians take for granted the large variety of grains they can choose from in order to meet the recommended servings. Having to follow a gluten-free diet for Celiac Disease or Dermatitis Herpetiformis limits the number of grain choices available.

Gluten is found in many cereal grains. The flour derived from these grains is what is traditionally used in baked goods. Gluten and its derivatives are also found in most commercially produced foods, including beer, dehydrated and canned soups, cream sauce mixes, some soya sauces, licorice and processed meats.

Once a diagnosis of Celiac Disease or Dermatitis Herpetiformis has been made, embracing a gluten-free diet is a challenge. It requires dedicated label reading and vigilance around food. Discovering just how extensive gluten is in our diet can be overwhelming. Many of the commercially available gluten-free baked items are expensive to buy and disappointing to eat. If a product label lists hydrolyzed vegetable protein (HVP), hydrolyzed plant protein (HPP), modified starch, soba pasta or vitamin and mineral supplements, there is the possibility of gluten in the product. Assuming a product is gluten free is *never* an option. Although it is difficult for some people to adjust to a gluten-free diet, a positive attitude helps immeasurably.

One of the challenges in complying with the gluten-free diet is the risk of cross-contamination. This occurs when gluten-containing food particles come in contact with gluten-free food. This easily happens in a household where regular and gluten-free diets coexist. If possible, set aside an area in your kitchen that remains gluten free. Toasters and shared spreads, jams, peanut butter, etc. are potential grounds for cross-contamination, so it is not uncommon for households to have doubles. Baking only with gluten-free flours eliminates the risk of cross-contamination. Eating away from home is an additional challenge. Even the most well-intentioned host may forget putting bread crumbs in the meatloaf, tossing croutons in the Caesar salad, or using a wheat starch–based baking powder in the otherwise gluten-free cake. Restaurant dining is another daunting endeavour. Many restaurants are unfamiliar with the specific requirements of a gluten-free diet.

Manufacturers have increased the supply and selection of gluten-free foods, much to the delight of those adhering to the diet. Gluten-free products are often readily available at large grocery stores. Consumers appreciate that these products are often labelled as gluten free. Disappointingly, many gluten-free baking mixes, cookies, snack foods and bakery items contain highly processed carbohydrates with little food value. Extra fats and sugars are sometimes added to enhance taste and extend shelf life. This creates a paradox for the newly diagnosed individual, who is often in poor health and in need of a highly nutritious diet.

For adherents of the gluten-free diet, the Canadian, American and worldwide Celiac Associations are vital support networks, as well as important resources for up-to-date information, newsletters, accurate diet and product research, and recipes. If you use other Internet sites for reference, make sure the source is credible.

GRAINS/FLOURS CONTAINING GLUTEN:

- » Barley
- » Bulgur
- » Dinkle
- » Durum
- » Einkorn
- » Emmer
- » Farro
- » Kamut
- » Oats (unless pure)
- » Rye
- » Spelt
- » Triticale
- » Wheat

WHAT MAKES GREAT GLUTEN-FREE FLOUR?

AMARANTH

» Amaranth was the staple food crop of the Aztecs for thousands of years. It is distantly related to beets, spinach and Swiss chard.

» The tan-coloured seed is a little larger than a poppy seed. It is easily milled in a coffee or spice grinder.

» Amaranth flour is a rich source of minerals and dietary fibre. It is a very good source of protein.

» The flour is an excellent binder. It produces dense, moist bread that withstands freezing. Its flavour is described as nutty. When the flour is not fresh it leaves an unpleasant aftertaste.

» The whole grain makes an excellent hot cereal.

» Store amaranth grain and flour in a sealed container in the freezer.

» 1 cup wheat flour is equal to 1 cup amaranth flour

BLACK, WHITE OR RED BEAN (CRANBERRY, KIDNEY, NAVY, PINTO, ROMANO)

(See page 20 for soy flour.)

» Beans are members of the legume family.

» They are an excellent source of protein, fibre and iron as well as a very good source of calcium.

» Bean flour yields a nicely browned, moist and slightly dense yeast bread. Use aged cheese, ripe banana, chocolate, instant coffee granules, flavouring extracts, molasses, peanut butter or spices to mask the flour's unpleasant taste and smell.

» Use only a small amount of the flour for a blend.

» The flour has a stable shelf life. Store away from heat and light.

» 1 cup wheat flour is equal to ¾ cup bean flour

BUCKWHEAT (LIGHT)

» Buckwheat is a staple of central Asia and parts of Eastern Europe. It is related to rhubarb and garden sorrel.

» The pyramid-shaped fruit of this plant is used as a grain.

» The flour is a good source of calcium, protein and fibre.

» The hulled buckwheat is referred to as groats. Toasted groats are called kasha (note that Kashi breakfast cereals are *not* gluten free).

» Milling buckwheat with the hull removed produces a beige, flecked flour. If a portion of the outside hull remains attached during milling, the flour is darker with a stronger flavour. Frequently this darker flour is lightened by the addition of enriched wheat flour. Check labels closely.

» The pure, light buckwheat flour has a mild flavour and excellent binding properties. It yields dense, slightly dry-textured bread, which lacks some visual appeal due to a faint purple hue. When buckwheat is combined in the GEMS flour this hue is not noticeable.

» Buckwheat flakes are an ideal oatmeal substitute. Coarsely ground buckwheat is available at most supermarkets. It is easily milled in a coffee or spice grinder.

» Coarsely ground buckwheat makes a tasty hot cereal.

» Buckwheat flour has a stable shelf life.

» 1 cup wheat flour is equal to ⅞ cup buckwheat flour

CHICKPEA (GARBANZO, CHANA, GRAM, BESAN)

» Chickpeas and chickpea flour are used extensively in the Middle East and India.
» Chickpeas are classified as a legume.
» Chickpea flour is an excellent source of protein and both soluble and insoluble fibre. It is a very good source of minerals and folic acid.
» The creamy yellow flour yields a light, moist bread with a soft and appealing texture.
» It has excellent binding properties. Chickpea flour has a mild aftertaste that usually disappears in a flour blend. Freezing increases this aftertaste. Chickpea flour has a stable shelf life.
» 1 cup wheat flour is equal to ¾ cup chickpea flour

CORN (MAIZE)

» Corn is indigenous to the Americas and comes in a variety of colours and grinds.
» Stone-ground cornmeal has good amounts of fibre and is a fair source of protein, vitamins and minerals.
» Regular cornmeal and corn flour have been stripped of nutrients, and then fortified with iron and B vitamins.
» Cornmeal has a pleasing texture and mild flavour.
» Baked goods are best served hot as they quickly become dry and crumbly. Cornmeal makes a delicious hot breakfast cereal.
» Store whole grain cornmeal/corn flour in a sealed container in the freezer. Regular cornmeal/corn flour has a stable shelf life.
» 1 cup wheat flour is equal to ⅞ cup corn flour

MILLET

» Millet was the staple of China before being displaced by rice. It provides a very good source of protein to millions of people in Africa and India.
» The seed resembles a mustard seed. The outside hull must be removed before it is edible. Millet is easily milled in a coffee or spice grinder.
» Nutritionally, millet is similar to wheat and is the most easily digested of all grains.
» The pale yellow flour yields bread that is light and soft with an appealing texture. It does have a mild aftertaste. It stays moist and has good binding properties. Freezing unfavourably changes the texture and binding properties of the bread.
» The cooked millet can be substituted for couscous.
» The seeds and flour deteriorate rapidly at room temperature.
» Store in a sealed container in freezer.
» 1 cup wheat flour is equal to 1 cup millet flour

MONTINA PURE BAKING SUPPLEMENT

(Do not confuse with Montina All-Purpose Flour Blend.)

» Montina is milled from the seed of a perennial plant called Indian ricegrass, which is native to North America.
» The Montina Pure Baking Supplement, made of 100 percent Indian ricegrass and produced by Amazing Grains in Montana, was developed specifically for the gluten-free diet. When it comes out of the box it resembles coarsely ground brown flax.
» Its protein and insoluble fibre content are very good.
» The Montina Pure Baking Supplement yields speckled, strongly flavoured bread with a gritty texture. It binds well and is moist.

» Use in amounts of 1 or 2 tablespoons in your baking if desired.

» Use the Pure Baking Supplement as you would flax.

» 1 cup wheat flour is equal to ½ cup Montina Pure Baking Supplement

OATS (PURE)

» Research has shown that small amounts of pure oats, uncontaminated by other grains, are safe to eat for individuals on a gluten-free diet. In Canada, pure oats have recently been reclassified and have received the endorsement of the Canadian Celiac Association.

» Sources for the pure oats are limited to health food stores or by mail order. As farmers learn new techniques for growing, storing and handling pure oats, the supply will gradually increase. Presently, all commercial oats available in grocery stores are contaminated with gluten-containing grains.

» Steel-cut oats result from the oat kernel being sliced once lengthwise. This particular style of oats, often used to make a hot cereal, is easily milled in a coffee or spice grinder.

» The beige-coloured flour contains good levels of protein, minerals and vitamins B and E. The nutrient-rich oat bran is a source of soluble and insoluble fibre.

» Oat flour has a pleasing flavour with a hint of sweetness. Its fibre content helps moisture retention. Combined with flours in a blend the flour yields a superb loaf of bread.

» Oats contain a natural preservative that extends shelf life.

» 1 cup wheat flour is equal to 1⅓ cups oat flour

QUINOA

» Quinoa (pronounced *keenwa*) is a grain the size of coarse sand. It grows at high altitudes in Peru and Ecuador and was revered by the Inca civilization.

» The outside bitter coating of the quinoa grain, saponin, acts as a natural pesticide. Rinse to remove residual coating left after processing.

» Quinoa has a similar amino acid profile to milk and holds the status of a "super grain." It is also an excellent source of magnesium and iron.

» The grain is easily milled in a coffee or spice grinder into a silky cream-coloured flour. The flour has excellent moisture and binding properties. Cakes prepared with the flour are delicate and freeze successfully.

» Use aged cheese, ripe banana, chocolate, instant coffee granules, flavouring extracts, molasses, peanut butter and spices to mask the flour's strong and distinct flavour. Use small amounts when preparing a blend. A flour blend mellows this flavour.

» The cooked form of the grain makes a nice addition to salads and casseroles. It is an excellent substitute for bulgur wheat.

» The seed and flour quickly go rancid. Store in a sealed container in the freezer.

» 1 cup wheat flour is equal to 1 cup quinoa flour

RICE (BROWN)

» Rice is the main source of food for a large percentage of the world's population.

» During processing, the outside hull is removed leaving the nutrient-rich bran. Further processing yields the familiar white rice.

» Brown rice flour has good amounts of protein and fibre. It is also a very good source of B vitamins, magnesium and zinc.

- » Most brown rice flour is milled from short or medium-length grain.
- » The flour yields mild-tasting bread that is appealing to the palate and binds well.
- » The texture of the bread made from this flour is moist and slightly dense. Its many favourable properties permit the flour to stand alone.
- » The recipes in *Gems of Gluten-Free Baking* can be made with brown rice flour, independent of other flours, with satisfactory results.
- » The flour can be kept at room temperature for up to a month. After a month the flour is subject to rancidity due to its oil content.
- » Store the bulk of brown rice flour in a sealed container in fridge or freezer.
- » 1 cup wheat flour is equal to ⅞ cup brown rice flour

SORGHUM (SWEET WHITE)

- » Sorghum is an Old World grain. It has been referred to as the poor man's millet. Historically it was a food source for India. It is the primary food source for Africa.
- » Sorghum is a good source of protein. It also is a fair source of calcium and iron.
- » A by-product of processing is sorghum molasses.
- » The sweet white variety of sorghum was developed for its milder flavour and lighter colour.
- » The tan, flecked flour yields wheat-like textured bread with cracking formations across the top.
- » The bread is slightly dry to the palate. Freezing alters texture and binding.
- » Sorghum has a stable shelf life.
- » 1 cup wheat flour is equal to 1 cup sorghum flour

SOY (LOW-FAT OR DEFATTED)

- » Soybeans, classified as legumes, have been used by the Chinese for thousands of years.
- » The protein is equivalent to meat in nutrient content.
- » The flour is an excellent source of fibre, minerals and vitamins.
- » Regular soy flour is a by-product of the process of extracting the natural oil from soybeans.
- » Low-fat soy flour is made from the soybean meal that remains after soybean oil is extracted. Defatted soy flour is further processed to remove all but 1 percent of the fat.
- » The flour yields a strongly flavoured bread that browns nicely, binds well and remains soft. Its moisture content enables it to freeze successfully.
- » Use aged cheese, ripe banana, chocolate, instant coffee granules, flavouring extracts, molasses, peanut butter or spices to mask its unpleasant flavour.
- » Use small amounts of the flour when preparing a blend.
- » Store the flour in a sealed container in freezer.
- » 1 cup wheat flour is equal to ¾ cup low-fat soy flour

TEFF

- » This ancient grain is the major food crop in Ethiopia and Eritrea.
- » Teff seed, the colour of brown flax, is similar in size to a poppy seed and classified as the smallest grain in the world. Teff means "lost" because so many of the seeds are lost during harvesting.
- » The flour is an excellent source of iron and fibre and a very good source of protein and calcium.

» Teff is arguably the most wheat-like in flavour of all the gluten-free whole grains. It is an excellent addition for any blend.

» The flour yields dense, chewy bread that binds well.

» The grain makes a delicious hot cereal.

» The grain has an extended shelf life.

» 1 cup wheat flour is equal to ⅞ cup teff flour

FLAX

» Although flax is not typically used as a flour, it is a whole grain used in baking.

» Flaxseed is a superb source of essential omega-3 fatty acid. According to the Flax Council of Canada, it is also is one of the richest sources of lignans (cancer-blocking compounds). Flaxseed is a valuable source of soluble and insoluble fibre.

Be sure and add a tablespoon or two of ground flax to your baking.

» Whole flaxseed can be stored at room temperature for well over a year. Keep it handy in the cupboard with your non-perishable baking supplies. Flaxseed is easily milled in a coffee or spice grinder. One Tbsp whole flaxseed equals 2 Tbsp ground. To ensure freshness and preserve quality, grind flaxseed just prior to using. Ground flax is also available in vacuum packed foil pouches. Once the bag is opened it is important to press out the air before resealing and storing in the fridge or freezer.

» A combination of 1 cup water, 2 Tbsp pure steel-cut oats, 1 Tbsp amaranth, 1 Tbsp teff and ½ tsp flaxseed yields a hot cereal that is a close facsimile of Red River or Sunny Boy cereal.

QUICK REFERENCE CHART:
NUTRITIOUS GLUTEN-FREE FLOURS

When whole grain is milled into flour, the bran (a source of fibre) and inner germ (the most nutritious part of the grain) are retained. Dietary fibre is found in most fruits, vegetables, legumes, grains, nuts and seeds. It is not digested or absorbed. There are two types of fibre, insoluble and soluble.

INSOLUBLE FIBRE absorbs water, making stools heavier and speeding their passage through the intestine. This helps prevent constipation.

SOLUBLE FIBRE forms a gel which interferes with the absorption of dietary fat and cholesterol and improves blood cholesterol levels.

FLOUR	ADVANTAGES	DRAWBACKS	USES/TIPS
AMARANTH	» very good source of protein » excellent source of insoluble fibre, calcium, magnesium and iron » pleasing taste and texture » retains moisture » good binding properties » baking freezes well	» mild nutty aftertaste » unpleasant aftertaste when flour is too old » slightly gritty texture » needs to be refrigerated	» excellent in a blend for breads, cookies, muffins and squares » used as a whole grain it makes a tasty hot breakfast cereal
BEAN White Black Red (Including cranberry, kidney, navy, pinto and romano bean flour)	» excellent source of protein, soluble and insoluble fibre » very good source of calcium » nice texture » adds tenderness to baking » good binding properties » baking freezes well » stable shelf life	» strong and unpleasant flavour and smell » density increased	» use in a blend for cakes, cupcakes, muffins, tea breads » reduce strong flavour with citrus zest, extracts, chocolate, coffee, spices, molasses, peanut butter
BUCKWHEAT (Light)	» very good source of protein, magnesium » good source of insoluble fibre » good binding properties » mild flavour » stable shelf life	» faint purple hue » dense somewhat dry texture » freezing increases dryness	» use in a blend for cookies, muffins, squares, breads » can use buckwheat flakes in place of oatmeal » coarsely ground buckwheat makes a tasty hot cereal
CHICKPEA Garbanzo Chana Gram Besan	» excellent source of protein, soluble and insoluble fibre » very good source of minerals » retains moisture, good binding properties » nice texture, stable shelf life » baking freezes well	» bright yellow colour » slight aftertaste	» excellent in a blend for cakes, cookies, squares, tea and yeast breads » use chickpea flour as a batter for deep fat frying » see recipe for Pistachio Cardamom Squares page 116

FLOUR	ADVANTAGES	DRAWBACKS	USES/TIPS
CORN	» good source of fibre » mild flavour » cornmeal adds pleasing texture » regular corn flour and cornmeal have stable shelf life	» texture is dry » baking dries out quickly » whole grain cornmeal and corn flour have a limited shelf life of 4 to 6 weeks » refrigerate for longer periods	» use in a blend for breads cookies, muffins, squares » use fine grind cornmeal for polenta, and medium grind for cornbread and muffins » makes a tasty hot cereal
MILLET	» nutritionally similar to wheat » very good source of protein, fibre » pleasing texture » retains moisture » baking is light and airy	» mild aftertaste » needs to be refrigerated » freezing significantly alters binding ability and palatability of breads	» excellent in a blend for cookies, muffins, squares, tea and yeast breads » gives bread products a wheat-like appearance and texture » grain is an excellent substitute for couscous
MONTINA	» very good source of protein, iron » excellent source of insoluble fibre » retains moisture » good binding properties » baking freezes well » stable shelf life	» strong, earthy taste » baked breads are dark and have a speckled appearance » not typically used as a flour	» use small amounts in baking where its drawbacks will not affect end result » do not confuse with Montina All-Purpose Flour Blend
OAT (Pure)	» good source of protein, minerals, B and E vitamins » excellent source of soluble and insoluble fibre » nice texture, mild flavour » retains moisture » baking freezes well » extended shelf life	» presently most commercial oats are contaminated » only oats certified as "pure" are guaranteed to be gluten free	» excellent in a blend for all baking » see recipe for Oatcakes page 84
QUINOA	» very good source of protein » good source of fibre » excellent source of iron and magnesium » retains moisture » nice texture	» strong and distinct flavour » needs to be refrigerated	» use in a blend for cupcakes-cakes, muffins, tea breads » reduce strong flavour with citrus zest, extracts, chocolate, coffee, spices, molasses, peanut butter » this grain is an excellent substitute for bulgur wheat
RICE (Brown)	» good source of protein » very good source of vitamins, magnesium, zinc » nice texture, mild flavour » retains moisture, light colour » good binding properties » most baking freezes well	» freezing alters binding ability » limited shelf life of 4 to 6 weeks without refrigeration	» primary flour in all GEMS flour blends » use flour separately for delicate baked goods (i.e., pastry, angel food cake, sugar cookies, etc.) » for sauces, rice and wheat are equivalent thickeners

FLOUR	ADVANTAGES	DRAWBACKS	USES/TIPS
SORGHUM (Sweet White)	» good source of protein, insoluble fibre » pleasing wheat-like texture » retains moisture » baking is light and airy » stable shelf life	» freezing alters texture and binding capacity of breads	» secondary flour in all GEMS flour blends » use in a blend for breads, cakes, muffins
SOY (Low-Fat, Defatted)	» excellent source of protein, soluble fibre » very good source of calcium, iron, magnesium » nice texture, browns well, retains moisture » good binding properties » baking freezes well	» strong unpleasant flavour » increases density » needs to be refrigerated	» use in a blend for general baking » reduce strong flavour with banana, herbs, extracts, citrus zest, chocolate, coffee, spices, molasses, peanut butter
TEFF	» very good source of protein » good source of insoluble fibre, calcium, iron, magnesium » chewy texture, mild flavour » retains moisture » good binding properties » baking freezes well » stable shelf life	» slightly gritty texture	» appealing brown colour » use in a blend for breads, cookies, muffins, squares » use flour separately for cookies and squares » the whole grain makes an excellent hot cereal

THE GEMS FLOUR

In a survey I conducted on gluten-free baking during the Calgary Celiac Association's 2006 Fall Conference, participants ranked bread products at the top of their list of disappointments. Attempts up to now to improve the status of gluten-free breads have not been fruitful.

A flour mix, consisting of starch and/or white rice flour, has generally been the only option available to those on a gluten-free diet. Starches are highly refined carbohydrates, void of vitamins, minerals and fibre. White rice has been stripped of its fibre and nutrient-rich bran prior to being milled into flour. Pea, sorghum, soy and brown rice flours are sometimes added to fortify this basic flour mix and improve its nutrient content. Baked items, breads in particular, prepared with this flour mix tend to be tasteless, dry and crumbly. I wanted to reverse this trend.

I began using brown rice flour for all my baking. It was familiar and nutritious, and produced satisfactory results. I gradually familiarized myself with other nutrient-rich gluten-free flours such as amaranth, buckwheat, chickpea and soy—13 flours in total. Baking with the flours individually helped me discover their distinctive characteristics. I used this information to create the GEMS flour.

The GEMS flour is a carefully selected blend of whole grain gluten-free flours with similar properties—colour, flavour, texture, moisture content, binding and freezing ability—to wheat flour. The GEMS flour yields bread that is delicious, moist and remains pleasing to consume even after 48 hours.

» 1 cup wheat flour is equal to 1 cup GEMS flour

GEMS FLOUR FORMULA

The value of this formula is that it tends to minimize the drawbacks and enhance the benefits of the individual flour. The formula requires four alternative gluten-free flours. The first two must be included; the next two offer a choice based on personal preference, availability or cost. All combinations will yield a superb loaf of bread:

BASIC	2¾ cups brown rice flour and ⅔ cup sweet white sorghum flour
ADD	⅓ cup of one of the following flours: amaranth, buckwheat (light), gluten-free oat or teff
ADD	3 Tbsp of one of the following flours: chickpea, millet, soy* (low-fat or defatted), quinoa* or white/red/black bean*

* Stronger-flavoured flour

Note: You may substitute regular sorghum flour (instead of sweet white) or regular buckwheat flour (instead of light) if necessary.

FORMULA BREAKDOWN

1. Brown rice flour is the primary flour for all combinations due to its light colour, mild flavour and versatility.
2. The sweet white sorghum flour lessens the density of brown rice flour, giving the loaf its bread-like appearance.
3. The amaranth, buckwheat (light), gluten-free oat and teff flours add texture and increase fibre. They also contribute binding properties.
4. The chickpea, millet, soy (low-fat or defatted), quinoa and white/red/black bean flours add tenderness and retain moisture.

Either a small or a large amount of GEMS flour can be made up at any given time. Keep 2 or 3 cups of GEMS flour handy in the cupboard and refrigerate the remainder. Remember all baking should be prepared with flour that is first brought to room temperature. The basic GEMS flour formula makes enough for two 8- × 4-inch loaves of bread.

Converting a Wheat Flour Recipe to a Gluten-Free Recipe:

1. Replace each cup of wheat flour with 1 cup GEMS flour.
2. Add ¼ to ½ tsp guar gum for each cup of flour.
3. Leavening agents: Double the amount of baking powder. Increase the baking soda by one-half the required amount. Double the amount of yeast.
4. Guar gum will thicken batter. Increase the volume of liquid called for in recipe by 2 Tbsp at a time until the desired consistency is obtained.

SUBSTITUTIONS

INGREDIENT	SUBSTITUTION
1 cup milk	» 1 cup of any of these non dairy-based beverages: almond, hemp, pure rice, vegetable or soy
1 cup buttermilk	» 1-Tbsp white vinegar or 1 Tbsp lemon juice + enough milk or milk beverage to equal 1 cup
1 cup sour cream	» ¾ cup silken tofu + 2 Tbsp vegetable oil » ¾ cup plain or soy yogurt + 2 Tbsp vegetable oil
¼ cup butter (Note: Recipes identified as "fat free" do not contain butter or oil, but may call for egg or dairy ingredients.)	» ¼ cup dairy-free butter spread » ¼ cup margarine » ¼ cup puréed prunes for use in chocolate recipes » ¼ cup applesauce for use in light-coloured baking » 3 Tbsp vegetable oil
1 whole egg	» 1½ tsp Ener-G powdered egg replacer + 2 Tbsp water » 2 egg whites » 1 Tbsp ground flax mixed with 3 Tbsp hot water » ½ tsp baking powder plus 3 Tbsp water
1 cup oatmeal	» 1 cup buckwheat flakes » ½ cup almond slices + ¼ cup millet flakes
1 tsp baking powder	» ¾ tsp cream of tartar + ¼ tsp baking soda » ¼ tsp baking soda + ½ tsp lemon juice
½ tsp cream of tartar	» 1 tsp pure white vinegar
1 cup granulated sugar	» 1 cup crystallized organic cane sugar (light gold in colour) » ¾ cup honey (affects browning characteristics so lower oven temperature by 25°F) » ¾ cup apple or white grape fuit juice concentrate less 3 Tbsp liquid from recipe » 1 cup sucralose, artifical sweetener made from table sugar (e.g., Splenda)

INGREDIENT	SUBSTITUTION
1 oz unsweetened chocolate	» 3 Tbsp cocoa + 1 Tbsp oil
1 oz semi-sweet chocolate	» 3 Tbsp cocoa + 1 Tbsp oil + 3 Tbsp granulated sugar
1 cup wheat flour	» 1 cup GEMS flour

PANTRY ESSENTIALS

Many adherents of the gluten-free diet stock their own non-perishables such as baking powder, baking soda, starch and sugar to eliminate a possible source of cross-contamination referred to as "double dipping." When sharing kitchen equipment with someone on a regular diet, be sure it is thoroughly washed and rinsed. Always do your gluten-free baking before baking with gluten-containing flours.

BINDERS: Guar gum, xanthan gum and methylcellulose are plant extracts referred to as binders. They act as a substitute for gluten and are interchangeable. These silky and cream-coloured binders increase the batter's viscosity, and its stabilizing and binding properties. The ratio I have found works the best is ½ tsp binder to 1 cup flour. Mix binder with flour before adding the liquid. Guar gum is the binder of choice in *Gems of Gluten-Free Baking*, as it is reasonably priced.

COFFEE GRINDER, SPICE GRINDER, HAND MILL: Use any of the above to grind amaranth, coarsely ground buckwheat, flax, millet, quinoa and steel-cut oats into a fine flour. On occasion you may have to regrind flour that feels too coarse, or when a recipe specifies finely ground flour.

FLOURS: Please refer to the individual flour in the section beginning on page 17.

NON-STICK COATING: The following mixture makes an excellent non-stick coating for bakeware: combine ¼ cup vegetable oil plus 2 Tbsp liquid soy lecithin in a small jar and blend until emulsified. Apply with a natural bristle pastry brush. Store with baking supplies. It is inexpensive, has an extended shelf life and does a superb job. I wouldn't be without it!

OILS & FATS: Use the vegetable oil of your choice. My preference is canola oil as it is a good source of monounsaturated fats. Salted butter is used for its flavour. Shortening is not used due to its trans fat content.

MEASURES: Measuring spoons include 1 Tbsp and 1, ½ and ¼ tsp measures. Nested measuring cups are used for dry ingredients and include ¼, ⅓, ½ and 1 cup measures. Measure liquids in glass or plastic with graduated markings and pouring spout. There is a slight distortion when taking measure at eye level, so read at the bottom of the surface's curve (the meniscus).

PANS: A clean tuna tin makes a suitably sized tin for a bun (ideal for making a bunwich). The 4-inch English muffin pans or crumpet rings make perfectly sized hamburger buns. An easy alternative would be to mould 4-inch reusable foil meat pie pans into a hamburger shape using a 28-ounce can of tomatoes as a template for the base. For hot dog buns mould and trim 5- × 3-inch reusable foil loaf pans. This requires a little patience and dexterity, but the results are worthwhile.

Having a variety of bakeware for breads, cakes, cookies, muffins, pies and tarts is necessary. If you need to purchase pans, buy good quality. It allows even heat distribution, does not bend out of shape and will last many years.

STARCHES: Highly processed carbohydrates classified as thickening agents, which include arrowroot, corn, potato and tapioca. Potato starch is derived from raw potatoes and potato flour from cooked potatoes. The two are not interchangeable. One Tbsp starch equals 2 Tbsp wheat flour.

SPRING-LOADED SCOOPS: Not essential but highly recommended, spring-loaded scoops are easy to use and less messy than scooping batter with a spoon. More importantly for some, cookies, muffins and pancakes will be uniform in size. The scoops come in 1, 2 and 4 Tbsp sizes. Add them to your wish list!

YEAST: There are two familiar types: the traditional active yeast and the instant or bread yeast. One can be substituted for the other. The traditional granular yeast is activated in a sugar/water solution for 5 or 10 minutes before being added to the dry ingredients. The instant or bread yeast is added directly to the dry ingredients.

Once opened, store yeast in the refrigerator. For occasional use, individual packets are available. The action of yeast benefits from the minerals in hard water. One tsp vinegar or lemon juice or a small pinch of ascorbic acid crystals (vitamin C) per cup of soft water can help correct water that is too soft. All yeast has an expiry date.

POINTERS FOR SUCCESS

Read through the entire recipe
to gauge time and steps involved in its preparation.

Have all ingredients
at hand before starting to make the recipe.

Dry ingredients and butter
should be at room temperature for baking.

All flours tend to settle in their containers.
Prior to measuring, stir with a fork or whisk
to aerate and lighten the flour.

To measure the flour correctly,
lightly spoon flour into a straight-sided measuring cup,
smoothe top with a straight-edged utensil and do not tap cup.

It is essential to mix the binding agent,
such as guar gum, with the dry ingredients
before adding any liquid.

Pack brown sugar into measuring cup
until it holds its shape when tipped out.

Preheat oven to the required temperature
about 20 minutes prior to baking.

Use the correct size of pan.

Turn pans 180 degrees for the last quarter
of baking time to ensure even browning. This step is not
necessary if you are using a convection oven.

CLOCKWISE FROM TOP: Pumpernickel Bread, page 40 •
Focaccia, page 44 • Fruit and Raisin Bread, page 39 •
Hamburger Buns, page 36 • Bread Sticks (left of Hamburger Buns), page 38

Yeast & Quick Breads

Currant Scones, page 53

YEAST AND QUICK BREADS

» Yeast breads are leavened with yeast. Quick breads are leavened with baking powder and/or baking soda balanced with an acidic ingredient.

» Some of the acidic ingredients that will neutralize the alkalinity in baking soda include buttermilk, yogurt, sour cream, cocoa, molasses, honey and citrus juice.

» Quick breads are best eaten fresh.

» Gluten-free bread is not as resilient as regular bread.

» Double-acting baking powder consists of baking soda, cream of tartar and cornstarch or wheat starch (check label). The baking soda reacts immediately when combined with an acid-based liquid. The baking powder requires heat to initiate its reaction.

» Gluten-free yeast dough does not require kneading or a second rising.

» Stale all-purpose bread can be used for poultry stuffing, bread pudding, Apple Brown Betty (page 186) or bread crumbs.

TIPS FOR SUCCESSFUL YEAST BREADS

1	Yeast is a microscopic plant. Under proper fermenting conditions traditional active dry yeast should produce a foam that will double in volume.
2	All yeast should have an expiry date noted on the package. See page 28 for information on types of yeast.
3	Cold inhibits the action of yeast. If you store your flour in the freezer allow it to come to room temperature first.
4	The elements in gluten give bread dough an elasticity that permits it to capture, expand and hold the carbon dioxide gas released from the fermentation process.
5	Gluten-free bread dough does rise but is unstable. The correct consistency of the bread dough is important (see next point). If too thin the bread will rise too quickly then collapse during baking. If the dough is too thick it will not rise. You will get an eye for the correct consistency.
6	The correct consistency of gluten-free bread dough resembles a thick cake batter. It should have a creamy, satiny appearance yet be able to hold a standing soup spoon.
7	If the dough appears to be too thick add 1 Tbsp of liquid at a time until you achieve the consistency desired.
8	If using a regular aluminum or glass bread pan grease only the bottom. The ungreased sides help the dough grip as it rises.
9	The top of the bread can be levelled with a spatula. Moisten your fingers with a little water to smoothe overtop. The binding agent (e.g., guar gum) prevents the dough from sticking to fingers.
10	Toppings such as sesame, poppy, mustard seeds, cheese, etc. adhere best when sprinkled overtop before bread begins to rise.
11	Let bread rise in a draft-free area such as toaster oven or microwave. My favourite is placing the loaf in a clear plastic bag with enough space to make a small dome (called "tenting").
12	Let dough rise to about ¼ inch below top rim of the pan—approximately 20 minutes. Place in a hot oven. The bread will rise a little further during the initial stages of baking.
13	Bread slices better the second day, otherwise the blade quickly gets gummy. A tomato knife works well if you have to cut a very fresh loaf of bread.
14	When humidity is low, bread will keep 2 to 3 days at room temperature. Bread that has not been frozen makes the best sandwiches. The same goes for hamburgers and hot dogs. Storing bread in the refrigerator accelerates the aging process.
15	For freezing, slice the complete loaf of bread. Slipping a piece of waxed paper between the slices facilitates easy retrieval once frozen.

BASIC ALL-PURPOSE BREAD

*This multi-purpose bread can be prepared
and baked within 1½ hours.*

2 cups GEMS flour

1 Tbsp ground flax

1 Tbsp instant yeast

1½ tsp guar gum

Scant 1 tsp salt

1⅓ cups lukewarm water

2 Tbsp vegetable oil

1 Tbsp honey or granulated sugar

1. Preheat oven to 375° F. Lightly grease bottom of an 8- × 4-inch loaf pan.
2. In mixing bowl mix GEMS flour, flax, yeast, guar gum and salt.
3. In separate bowl blend water, oil and honey or sugar.
4. Pour liquids into dry ingredients and beat to a creamy, thick consistency with hand mixer.
5. Spoon dough evenly into prepared pan and smoothe top with moistened fingers.
6. Let dough rise in a draft-free area to ¼ inch from top of pan for approximately 20 minutes.
7. Bake in centre of oven for 30 to 35 minutes.
8. Turn bread out of pan and cool on rack.

YIELD: One 8- × 4-inch loaf

EGG & DAIRY FREE

HAMBURGER BUNS

Now you can enjoy a real "hamburger."

Prepare recipe for Basic All-Purpose Bread, page 35.

1. Preheat oven to 350°F. Lightly grease pans (see Pantry Essentials, page 27) and place on baking sheet.
2. Spoon ½ cup dough into each pan (or ⅓ cup for a thinner bun). Sprinkle with sesame seeds if desired. Let rise 15 to 18 minutes.
3. Bake 20 minutes. Cool 5 minutes before turning out of pans.

YIELD: 5 hamburger buns

EGG & DAIRY FREE

Pictured on page 30

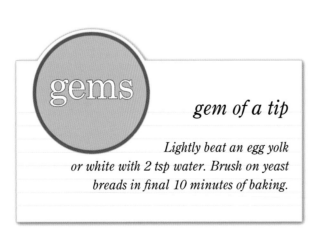

gems

gem of a tip

Lightly beat an egg yolk or white with 2 tsp water. Brush on yeast breads in final 10 minutes of baking.

BUNWICHES OR HOT DOG BUNS

The bunwich is the perfect size for work or school.

Prepare recipe for Basic All-Purpose Bread, page 35.

1. Preheat oven to 350°F. Lightly grease pans (see Pantry Essentials, page 27) and place on baking sheet.
2. Spoon ⅓ cup dough into each (or ¼ cup for a thinner bun). Let rise 15 minutes.
3. Bake 18 minutes. Cool 5 minutes before turning out of pans.

YIELD: 7 bunwiches or 7 hot dog buns

EGG & DAIRY FREE

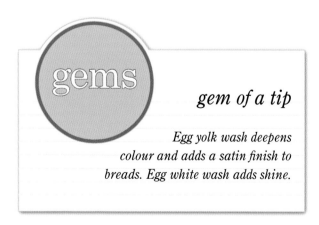

gems

gem of a tip

Egg yolk wash deepens colour and adds a satin finish to breads. Egg white wash adds shine.

BREAD STICKS

Please read through all of the instructions before you start.
Store in airtight container to keep crisp.

2 Tbsp Parmesan cheese
1 Tbsp each sesame seeds and dried onion
   flakes

½ Tbsp each poppy seeds, cornmeal and
   coarse salt

1. Cut a piece of baking parchment to fit a 9- × 15-inch baking sheet. With the shorter
    end facing you, draw a horizontal line across the top, 1 inch from the edge, using a
    ruler and coloured pencil. Draw another horizontal line directly 6 inches below.
2. Between the two horizontal lines draw six 6-inch vertical lines 1 inch apart.
3. Repeat the above, drawing six more lines at the opposite end. Turn the paper over
    and place on baking sheet. Lines must be clearly visible through the paper.
4. In a 1-cup measure, mix the Parmesan, sesame seeds, dried onion flakes, poppy
    seeds, cornmeal and coarse salt.
5. Using a ¼ tsp measure or a small spoon, trail a bit of the seed mixture down each
    vertical line. Set remainder aside.
6. Preheat oven to 400°F. In small bowl prepare a half recipe of Basic All-Purpose
    Bread (page 35).
7. Place dough in a 2-cup plastic bag. Snip ⅓ inch off one corner. Close the bag tightly
    and squeeze strips of dough down each vertical line. Use the ¼ tsp measure to
    sprinkle the remaining seed mix down each bread stick. (I find the mixture
    adheres best if you sprinkle it on immediately after each strip is squeezed out.)
    Rising is not necessary.
8. Place in the centre of the oven and bake 10 minutes. Turn the bread sticks over,
    then bake a further 10 minutes. Shut off the oven, leaving in the bread sticks to
    dry out. (For really crunchy bread sticks, wait until the oven cools down completely.)

YIELD: 12 bread sticks

EGG FREE

Pictured on page 30

FRUIT AND RAISIN BREAD

This is as delicious to eat as it is to look at.

1 cup GEMS flour
1 cup brown rice flour
1 Tbsp plus 1 tsp instant yeast
1½ tsp guar gum
1 tsp salt
1⅓ cups lukewarm water
2 Tbsp vegetable oil
2 Tbsp liquid honey or granulated sugar

½ cup sultana raisins, coarsely chopped
¼ cup chopped glacé fruitcake mix

ICING
Combine in a small bowl: ½ cup icing sugar,
2 tsp water, ½ tsp white corn syrup
and ¼ tsp vanilla extract or ⅛ tsp almond
extract and mix until smooth.

1. Preheat oven to 375°F. Lightly grease bottom of 8- × 4-inch loaf pan.
2. In mixing bowl blend GEMS flour, brown rice flour, yeast, guar gum and salt.
3. In separate bowl combine the water, oil and honey or sugar.
4. Add wet ingredients to dry ingredients and beat to a creamy, thick consistency with hand mixer. Stir in raisins and fruit.
5. Spoon dough evenly into prepared pan and smoothe top with moistened fingers.
6. Let rise in a draft-free area to ¼ inch from top of pan.
7. Bake 30 to 35 minutes.
8. Turn bread out of pan and place right side up on rack. Drizzle icing overtop and down sides while warm.

YIELD: One 8- × 4-inch loaf

EGG & DAIRY FREE

Pictured on page 30

PUMPERNICKEL BREAD

Enjoy with smoked meat, sauerkraut and Dijon mustard.

1¾ cups GEMS flour

½ cup bean flour

1 Tbsp plus 1 tsp instant yeast

1 Tbsp cocoa

2 tsp caraway seeds

1 Tbsp ground flax

1½ tsp guar gum

1 tsp salt

1⅔ cups lukewarm water

3 Tbsp vegetable oil

2 Tbsp molasses

1 Tbsp brown sugar

¼ tsp finely grated orange zest

Caraway seeds for sprinkling overtop

1. Preheat oven to 375°F. Lightly grease bottom of a 6-inch round pan.
2. In mixing bowl blend GEMS flour, bean flour, yeast, cocoa, caraway and flax, guar gum and salt.
3. In separate container blend water, oil, molasses, brown sugar and orange zest.
4. Add wet ingredients to dry ingredients and beat to a creamy, thick consistency with hand mixer.
5. Spoon dough evenly into prepared pan and smoothe top with moistened fingers. Sprinkle 1 tsp of caraway seeds overtop.
6. Let dough rise in a draft-free area to ¼ inch from top of pan.
7. Bake 30 to 35 minutes.
8. Place on rack and cool 5 minutes before turning out of pan.

YIELD: One 6-inch round loaf

EGG & DAIRY FREE

Pictured on page 30

HEARTY COUNTRY BREAD

This bread has a wonderful flavour and rich colour.

1⅓ cups GEMS flour
⅓ cup gluten-free quick oats
1½ Tbsp instant yeast
3 Tbsp coarsely ground walnuts
1 Tbsp ground sunflower seeds
1 Tbsp ground flax
1½ tsp guar gum

1 tsp salt
1⅓ cups lukewarm water
2 Tbsp vegetable oil
2 Tbsp molasses
1 Tbsp brown sugar
Gluten-free quick oats for
   sprinkling overtop

1. Preheat oven to 400°F. Lightly grease bottom of an 8- × 4-inch loaf pan.
2. In mixing bowl combine GEMS flour, oats, yeast, walnuts, sunflower seeds, flax, guar gum and salt.
3. Blend the water, oil, molasses and brown sugar.
4. Add liquid ingredients to the dry ingredients and beat to a creamy, thick consistency with hand mixer.
5. Spoon dough into prepared pan and level. Smoothe top with moistened fingers. Sprinkle oats overtop.
6. Let dough rise in a draft-free area to ¼ inch from top of pan.
7. Bake 10 minutes at set temperature then lower to 325°F and bake a further 25 to 30 minutes.
8. Place on rack and cool 5 minutes before turning out of pan to finish cooling.

YIELD: One 8- × 4-inch loaf

EGG & DAIRY FREE

CLASSIC SOURDOUGH BREAD

Sourdough is one of the oldest styles of bread.

SOURDOUGH STARTER

This starter requires 4 days to ferment (do not use if it smells foul or has a pink tinge).

1⅛ tsp traditional active dry yeast
1¼ cups brown rice flour
1¼ cups lukewarm water

1. In glass bowl, combine the yeast and ¼ cup of the lukewarm water. Let stand until bubbles start to rise, about 5 to 10 minutes.
2. Stir in the flour and remaining water and mix to combine.
3. Pour into a 4-cup glass jar and cover with two or three layers of cheesecloth or other porous material (air exchange is necessary in order to achieve the correct sourdough flavour).
4. Let stand for 4 days in a warm place, about 75°F to 80°F (I keep mine in a cupboard above the stove). Do not stir.
5. After 4 days, starter can either be used immediately or stored in a sealed container in the refrigerator for up to 10 days.

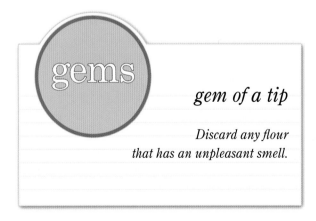

gems

gem of a tip

Discard any flour that has an unpleasant smell.

SOURDOUGH BREAD

1⅛ tsp traditional active dry yeast

¼ tsp granulated sugar

½ cup lukewarm water

1 cup sourdough starter

Scant tsp salt

¾ cup brown rice flour

½ cup GEMS flour

1½ tsp guar gum

Cornmeal for sprinkling pan bottom

1. Lightly grease bottoms of two 6-inch round pans and sprinkle each pan with cornmeal.
2. In mixing bowl dissolve yeast and sugar in lukewarm water and let stand until bubbles start to rise, 5 to 10 minutes.
3. Stir in the sourdough starter, salt, brown rice flour, GEMS flour and guar gum and beat until creamy and thick with hand mixer.
4. Spoon dough evenly into prepared pans. Smoothe tops with moistened fingers.
5. Let dough rise in draft-free area for 70 to 80 minutes.
6. Preheat oven to 425°F during the last 20 minutes of the bread's rising time.
7. Bake 15 minutes, than lower heat to 350°F and bake a further 10 minutes. For a chewier crust spray a fine mist of water on the bread two or three times during baking.
8. Place on rack and cool 5 minutes before turning out of pan to finish cooling.

YIELD: Two 6-inch round loaves

EGG, DAIRY & FAT FREE

FOCACCIA BREAD

Fresh herbs intensify flavour (1 Tbsp
of a freshly chopped herb equals 1 tsp dried).

1¾ cups GEMS flour
1 Tbsp instant yeast
2 tsp crumbled dried rosemary
1½ tsp granulated sugar
¾ tsp salt
½ tsp guar gum
2 garlic cloves, crushed
2 Tbsp olive oil
1¼ cups lukewarm water
¼ cup coarsely chopped sun-dried
  tomatoes
Olive oil to brush overtop

Cornmeal for sprinkling on bottom of pan

TOPPING
Combine 1 tsp rosemary, 1 tsp Italian Herb
  Mix, 1 tsp coarse salt and ½ tsp coarsely
  ground pepper.

NOTE
To make Italian Herb Mix, combine 2 tsp
  oregano and 1 tsp each marjoram, thyme
  and basil.

1. Preheat oven to 425°F. Lightly grease an 8-inch round pan. Sprinkle bottom with cornmeal.
2. In mixing bowl blend GEMS flour, yeast, rosemary, sugar, salt and guar gum and set aside.
3. In small skillet sauté garlic in oil until aromatic. Combine with water and pour into flour mixture. Beat to a creamy, thick consistency with hand mixer. Stir in sun-dried tomatoes.
4. Spoon into prepared pan and level top. Moisten index finger and press dimple-like indentations 2 inches apart into dough. Sprinkle with topping mixture.
5. Let rise in a draft-free area about 30 minutes. Bake 20 to 25 minutes.
6. Remove from oven and brush with olive oil. Turn out of pan and place on rack to cool.

YIELD: One 8-inch round loaf

EGG & DAIRY FREE

Pictured on page 30

CHEESE BREAD

Toasting the bread accentuates the cheese flavour.

1 cup brown rice flour

¾ cup GEMS flour

1 Tbsp plus 1 tsp instant yeast

1½ tsp guar gum

½ tsp salt

½ cup coarsely grated extra old cheddar
cheese (reserve 2 Tbsp for topping)

⅓ cup Parmesan cheese

1⅓ cups lukewarm water

2 Tbsp tomato paste for colour (optional)

1. Preheat oven to 375°F. Lightly grease bottom of an 8- × 4-inch loaf pan.
2. In mixing bowl blend brown rice flour, GEMS flour, yeast, guar gum, salt, 6 Tbsp cheddar and Parmesan cheeses and set aside.
3. Combine water and tomato paste (if using) and add to flour mixture. Beat to a creamy, thick consistency with hand mixer.
4. Spoon into prepared pan and level. Smoothe top with moistened fingers. Sprinkle with the reserved 2 Tbsp cheese.
5. Let dough rise in a draft-free place to ¼ inch from top of pan.
6. Bake 30 to 35 minutes. Turn bread out of pan and cool right side up on rack.

YIELD: One 8- × 4-inch loaf

EGG FREE

BUTTERY DINNER ROLLS

Rich and flavourful!

1 cup brown rice flour
¾ cup GEMS flour
1 Tbsp instant yeast
1½ tsp guar gum

½ tsp salt
1¼ cups lukewarm milk
3 Tbsp melted butter
2½ Tbsp granulated sugar

1. Preheat oven to 375°F. Lightly grease 8 to 10 muffin cups.
2. In mixing bowl blend brown rice flour, GEMS flour, yeast, guar gum and salt.
3. In separate bowl combine milk, butter and sugar.
4. Pour milk mixture into dry ingredients and beat to a creamy, thick consistency with hand mixer.
5. Drop ¼ cup batter into each muffin cup, or make cloverleaf buns by dropping three 1½ Tbsp dollops of dough into each muffin cup with small spring-loaded scoop.
6. Let rise in a draft-free area for 30 to 35 minutes.
7. Bake for 15 to 18 minutes.
8. Cool buns on rack a few minutes before removing from pan.

YIELD: 8 dinner rolls or 10 cloverleaf buns

EGG FREE

BUTTERSCOTCH KNOTS

These are delectable.

1 cup brown rice flour

⅔ cup GEMS flour

1 Tbsp instant yeast

1½ tsp guar gum

½ tsp salt

1 cup plus 3 Tbsp lukewarm water

2 Tbsp vegetable oil

2 Tbsp liquid honey or granulated sugar

¼ cup melted butter

PUDDING/NUT MIXTURE

In a small bowl combine ¼ cup butterscotch or vanilla gluten-free pudding powder (not instant), 6 Tbsp brown sugar, ¼ cup chopped pecans, ½ tsp cinnamon. Set aside.

1. Preheat oven to 350°F. Grease 9 muffin cups well.
2. In mixing bowl blend brown rice flour, GEMS flour, yeast, guar gum and salt.
3. In separate bowl combine water, oil and honey or sugar.
4. Pour liquid mixture into dry ingredients and beat to a creamy, thick consistency with hand mixer.
5. Place 1 tsp melted butter in each muffin cup. Sprinkle with 1 Tbsp pudding/nut mixture.
6. Spoon 3 Tbsp of dough into each cup. Sprinkle with more of the pudding/nut mixture.
7. Let rise 20 minutes in a draft-free area. Bake 15 minutes. Cool 20 minutes. Turn out of pan onto parchment paper to finish cooling.

YIELD: 9 butterscotch knots

EGG FREE

HOT CROSS BUNS

A traditional symbolic sweet roll served each spring.

1½ cups GEMS flour
1 Tbsp instant yeast
1¼ tsp guar gum
1 tsp salt
1 tsp ground cinnamon
¼ tsp ground nutmeg
1⅛ cup warm milk
⅓ cup granulated sugar
2 Tbsp melted butter

⅓ cup currants
¼ cup glacé fruitcake mix

ICING

Mix ½ cup icing sugar, 1 tsp milk, ¼ tsp vanilla extract. Place mixture in a small plastic bag, snip a tiny corner and squeeze the mixture gently out of the bag to form a cross on each bun.

1. Preheat oven to 350° F. Lightly grease a muffin tin.
2. In mixing bowl blend GEMS flour, yeast, guar gum, salt, cinnamon and nutmeg.
3. In a 2-cup measure combine the milk, sugar and butter. Add to dry ingredients and beat to a thick, creamy consistency with hand mixer. Stir in currants and fruit.
4. Spoon ¼ cup of dough into each muffin cup.
5. Let rise 45 minutes in a draft-free area.
6. Bake 15 to 18 minutes. Remove to rack.
7. Apply icing while buns are warm.

YIELD: 8 buns

EGG FREE

GLAZED CINNAMON ROLLS

These are finicky. Give yourself time to master the technique.

1¼ cups brown rice flour
½ cup GEMS flour
3 Tbsp granulated sugar
½ cup sultana raisins
1 Tbsp instant yeast
¼ cup granulated sugar
1½ tsp guar gum
¾ tsp ground cinnamon

½ tsp salt
¾ cup plus 2 Tbsp lukewarm water
½ cup melted butter, cooled

GLAZE
In microwave heat 1 Tbsp milk and
1 Tbsp sugar for 30 seconds to
dissolve the sugar.

1. Line bottom of an 11- × 7- × 2-inch oblong pan with parchment paper and lightly grease sides. Also lightly grease bottom of an 8- × 5- × 2-inch pan.
2. In mixing bowl blend brown rice flour, GEMS flour, yeast, sugar, guar gum, cinnamon and salt. Combine water and butter then add to dry ingredients, beating with hand mixer until a creamy, thick consistency.
3. Spread dough evenly over bottom of larger pan. Distribute raisins. Combine sugar and cinnamon and sprinkle overtop. Cover with plastic wrap and gently press wrap into dough to ensure raisins and sugar adhere. Chill in refrigerator for 1 hour to firm up but not become hard.
4. Grasping parchment paper at one end of pan slide dough-lined paper onto counter. Beginning at one end, slip spatula between paper and dough. With a rolling motion of spatula begin forming a roll, lifting the parchment to help guide and support the rolling. Moisten fingers to assist in shaping and keeping the roll tight. Discard parchment paper.
5. Preheat oven to 375°F.
6. With a sharp knife slice into six rolls and place in the smaller prepared pan. Cover lightly and let rise 15 minutes. Bake 30 minutes. Five minutes before removing from oven apply glaze with pastry brush. Place on rack to cool.

YIELD: 6 rolls

EGG FREE

Pictured on the back cover

SAVOURY CHEESE BISCUITS

Omit the cheese and use the biscuits to top a stew.

1 cup brown rice flour
½ cup GEMS flour
1 Tbsp baking powder
½ tsp guar gum
¼ tsp salt
3 Tbsp cold butter, diced or grated

½ cup grated sharp cheddar cheese
  (reserve 2 Tbsp for topping)
1½ tsp each chopped fresh green onions
  and parsley
⅔ cup milk
Brown rice flour for work surface

1. Preheat oven to 450°F. Lightly grease 8- × 8-inch pan.
2. In mixing bowl blend brown rice flour, GEMS flour, baking powder, guar gum and salt.
3. Add butter and work into flour mixture with pastry blender or fingers. Mix in the 6 Tbsp cheese and herbs to combine.
4. Pour milk into flour and cheese mixture mixing enough to form a ball.
5. Turn dough out on lightly floured surface and pat to a 1-inch thickness. Cut dough into 2-inch circles (an upside-down drinking glass works well for this). Sprinkle with the reserved 2 Tbsp cheese.
6. Bake about 15 minutes. Serve hot.

YIELD: 7 biscuits

EGG FREE

IRISH SODA BREAD

Legend says the X cut into the top wards off evil spirits.

Brown rice flour for pan
1 cup GEMS flour
¼ cup gluten-free quick oats
2 Tbsp ground flax
1 tsp baking soda

¼ tsp salt
½ tsp guar gum
2 Tbsp cold butter, diced into small pieces
  or grated
¾ cup plain, low-fat yogurt

1. Preheat oven to 425°F. Lightly grease baking sheet and sprinkle it with brown rice flour in a 6-inch circle.
2. In mixing bowl combine GEMS flour, oats, flax, baking soda, salt and guar gum.
3. Mix in the butter using pastry blender or fingers until blended.
4. Stir in yogurt, mixing enough to form a soft ball.
5. Turn dough out onto lightly floured pan and gently pat into a 6-inch disk.
6. With a sharp knife cut an X ½ inch deep in the centre of the disk. Sprinkle top with a little rice flour.
7. Bake about 20 minutes.
8. Best served directly out of the oven.

YIELD: One 6-inch round loaf

EGG FREE

BUCKWHEAT KASHA BREAD

This hearty coarse-textured quick bread has satisfying appeal.

¼ cup coarsely ground buckwheat, toasted
⅓ cup boiling water
1 cup light buckwheat flour
¾ cup GEMS flour
½ cup ground hazelnuts
⅓ cup brown sugar

2 tsp baking powder
2 tsp baking soda
½ tsp salt
1¼ cups buttermilk
¼ cup vegetable oil

1. Toast the buckwheat in small frying pan to darken slightly (once toasted it is referred to as kasha). Combine the kasha with the boiling water and let stand 15 minutes.
2. Preheat oven to 350°F. Lightly grease 8- × 4-inch loaf pan.
3. In medium-sized mixing bowl blend flours, ground nuts, brown sugar, baking powder, baking soda and salt.
4. In a small bowl whisk buttermilk, oil and kasha/water mixture. Add to dry ingredients and beat lightly until blended.
5. Spoon evenly into prepared pan. It will be full. Bake 50 to 60 minutes. Cool in pan 20 minutes before turning out on rack to cool.

YIELD: One 8- × 4-inch loaf

EGG FREE

CURRANT SCONES

Traditionally served at afternoon tea with a dollop of Devon cream.

Brown rice flour for pan
1½ cups brown rice flour
3 Tbsp granulated sugar
3 tsp baking powder
¼ tsp baking soda
⅓ tsp ground nutmeg
½ tsp guar gum
Pinch salt
3 Tbsp cold butter
⅔ cup buttermilk

⅓ cup plain yogurt
½ cup currants
Coarsely granulated sugar for sprinkling
  on top

VARIATION
Replace the nutmeg and currants with
  coarsely chopped dried cranberries
  and zest of one orange.

1. Preheat oven to 375°F. Lightly grease a baking sheet. Sprinkle brown rice flour on it in a 6-inch circle.
2. In mixing bowl blend 1½ cups brown rice flour, sugar, baking powder, baking soda, nutmeg, guar gum and salt.
3. Using pastry blender or fingers cut butter into flour to resemble a coarse meal. Mix in currants.
4. Combine buttermilk and yogurt. Add to dry ingredients stirring just enough to moisten. With spatula, shape into a soft ball.
5. Turn dough out onto prepared sheet and pat into a 6-inch dish. Sprinkle with sugar.
6. Bake 20 minutes. When cool cut into six wedges. Serve same day.

YIELD: 6 scones

EGG FREE

Pictured on page 32

STOLLEN

The ricotta cheese keeps this delicious quick bread moist.

2 cups GEMS flour
⅓ cup granulated sugar
1 Tbsp baking powder
1 tsp guar gum
¼ tsp salt
6 Tbsp cold butter, diced
½ tsp lemon zest
½ cup glacé fruitcake mix
½ cup light or dark raisins

⅓ cup toasted slivered almonds
1 cup ricotta cheese
1 egg
1 tsp vanilla extract

GLAZE
Mix 1 cup icing sugar, 1½ Tbsp milk and
⅛ tsp almond extract to spreading
consistency.

1. Preheat oven to 325°F. Lightly grease one large baking sheet.
2. In mixing bowl blend GEMS flour, sugar, baking powder, guar gum and salt. Add butter and work with fingers until mixture resembles coarse cornmeal. Stir in the zest, chopped fruits, raisins and nuts until combined.
3. In small bowl blend ricotta cheese, egg and vanilla. Add to dry ingredients and mix until most of flour is moistened.
4. Turn out dough onto floured surface and lightly roll two or three times with your hands. Divide into two balls.
5. Roll each ball into a 7- × 6-inch oval, ½ inch thick. Fold each piece not quite in half and place on prepared pan.
6. Bake 35 to 40 minutes. Cool a few minutes before spreading on the glaze.

YIELD: 2 stollen

CHEESE AND ONION CORNBREAD

Wonderful flavour and easy to make.

1 large onion, thinly sliced
1 Tbsp vegetable oil
1¼ cups GEMS flour
¾ cup cornmeal
¼ soy flour
1 Tbsp baking powder
1 tsp granulated sugar

1 tsp salt
1½ cups coarsely grated sharp
   cheddar cheese
1 cup milk
2 eggs
2 Tbsp vegetable oil

1. Sauté onions in the 1 Tbsp oil for 15 minutes stirring frequently. Cool.
2. Preheat oven to 350° F. Lightly grease 9- × 5-inch loaf pan.
3. In mixing bowl combine GEMS flour, cornmeal, soy flour, baking powder, sugar and salt.
4. Stir in the cheese and mix well.
5. In another bowl, combine milk, eggs and oil and beat until blended.
6. Pour contents of liquid mixture into centre of dry ingredients and mix just enough to moisten flours.
7. Spoon into prepared pan and smoothe evenly. Distribute onions across the top.
8. Bake for 45 minutes. Serve warm.

YIELD: One 9- × 5-inch loaf

Rhubarb Streusel Muffins, page 66

Muffins & Tea Breads

Spicy Pumpkin Bread, page 73

MUFFINS AND TEA BREADS

» The main difference between muffins and tea breads is the pans used. The ingredients and method for preparing either are similar, although baking times vary.

» A tea bread recipe using 1½ to 2 cups flour yields 12 regular-sized muffins.

» A recipe using 1½ cups flour requires an 8- x 4-inch loaf pan. If more than 2 cups flour are called for a 9- x 5-inch loaf pan is necessary.

» The key to success with muffins and tea breads is to mix the batter just long enough to moisten all the dry ingredients.

» Muffins have a coarser texture and are not as sweet as cupcakes. Tea breads taste and slice better the day after they are baked.

» For smaller loaves, ideal for freezing, replace one 9- x 5- x 3-inch loaf pan with three 5- x 3- x 2-inch pans, or one 8- x 4-inch pan with two 5- x 3- x 2-inch pans.

APRICOT ORANGE MUFFINS

Easy, moist and absolutely delicious!

1½ cups GEMS flour
⅓ cup granulated sugar
1 Tbsp baking powder
1 tsp baking soda
½ tsp guar gum
½ tsp salt
⅛ tsp ground nutmeg

3 Tbsp vegetable oil
1 egg
1 tsp vanilla extract
1 tsp grated orange zest
¾ cup orange juice
½ cup chopped dried apricots
½ cup sultana raisins

1. Preheat oven to 350°F. Lightly grease muffin tin.
2. In mixing bowl blend GEMS flour, sugar, baking powder, baking soda, guar gum, salt and nutmeg. Make a well in the centre.
3. In separate bowl whisk together the oil, egg, vanilla, zest and juice.
4. Pour orange juice mixture into well and stir until ingredients are just moistened. Stir in apricots and raisins.
5. Spoon ¼ cup batter into each muffin cup.
6. Bake 20 minutes or until springy to touch. Place on rack to cool.

YIELD: 1 dozen

DAIRY FREE

BANANA NUT MUFFINS

Quick and easy to prepare.

1¼ cups GEMS flour
½ cup gluten-free quick oats
1 Tbsp ground flax
⅓ cup brown sugar
2 tsp baking powder
1 tsp baking soda
½ tsp salt

¼ tsp guar gum
3 Tbsp vegetable oil
1 egg
¾ cup milk
½ cup very ripe mashed banana (1 large)
⅓ cup chopped walnuts

1. Preheat oven to 350°F. Lightly grease muffin tin.
2. In mixing bowl blend GEMS flour, oats, flax, brown sugar, baking powder, baking soda, salt and guar gum and make a well in the centre.
3. In a separate bowl whisk together the oil, egg, milk and banana.
4. Pour banana mixture into well and stir until ingredients are just moistened, adding the nuts last.
5. Spoon ¼ cup batter into each muffin cup.
6. Bake 20 minutes or until springy to touch. Place on rack to cool.

YIELD: 1 dozen

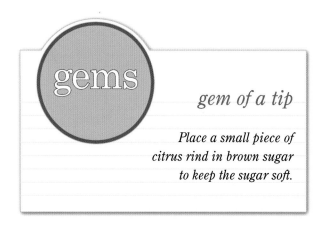

gems

gem of a tip

*Place a small piece of
citrus rind in brown sugar
to keep the sugar soft.*

BERRY CREAM MUFFINS

These have taste and eye appeal.

1½ cups brown rice flour

⅔ cup granulated sugar (reduce the sugar
   to ½ cup if using just blueberries)

1 Tbsp baking powder

½ tsp baking soda

½ tsp guar gum

½ tsp salt

2 Tbsp vegetable oil

1 egg

½ tsp vanilla extract

1¼ cups light sour cream

1 cup blueberries and ½ cup raspberries
   (fresh or frozen)

1. Preheat oven to 350°F. Lightly grease muffin tin.
2. In mixing bowl blend brown rice flour, sugar, baking powder, baking soda, guar gum and salt. Make a well in the centre.
3. In separate bowl whisk together the oil, egg, vanilla and sour cream.
4. Pour sour cream mixture into well and stir until dry ingredients are just moistened. Fold in berries.
5. Spoon ¼ cup batter into each muffin cup.
6. Bake 20 to 25 minutes or until springy to touch. Place on rack to cool.

YIELD: 1 dozen

CHOCOLATE APPLESAUCE MUFFINS

The applesauce keeps these chocolatey muffins extra moist.

1½ cup GEMS flour
½ cup granulated sugar
¼ cup cocoa
1 Tbsp ground flax
1 Tbsp baking powder
1 tsp baking soda
¾ tsp guar gum
½ tsp salt

¼ cup vegetable oil
1 egg
½ cup unsweetened applesauce
¾ cup buttermilk
½ tsp vanilla extract
⅓ cup chocolate chips (dark or white chocolate)

1. Preheat oven to 375°F. Lightly grease muffin tin.
2. In mixing bowl blend GEMS flour, sugar, cocoa, flax, baking powder, baking soda, guar gum and salt. Make a well in the centre.
3. In separate bowl whisk together oil, egg, applesauce, buttermilk and vanilla.
4. Pour applesauce mixture into well and stir until dry ingredients are just moistened. Add chocolate chips.
5. Spoon ¼ cup batter into each muffin cup.
6. Bake 18 minutes or until springy to touch. Place on rack to cool.

YIELD: 1 dozen

CORNMEAL MUFFINS

These light, slightly sweet muffins are best right after baking.

1¼ cups milk

¾ cup cornmeal

1 cup GEMS flour

3 Tbsp granulated sugar

1 Tbsp baking powder

½ tsp salt

½ tsp guar gum

1 egg

3 Tbsp vegetable oil

½ cup grated cheddar cheese (optional)

1. Preheat oven to 350°F. Lightly grease muffin tin or 8- × 8-inch pan.
2. In small bowl blend milk and cornmeal and set aside for 5 minutes.
3. In mixing bowl blend GEMS flour, sugar, baking powder, salt and guar gum. Make a well in the centre.
4. Blend egg and oil into milk and cornmeal mixture.
5. Pour milk mixture into well and stir until dry ingredients are just moistened.
6. Spoon ¼ cup batter into each muffin cup or pour batter into a prepared pan. Sprinkle cheddar cheese overtop if desired.
7. Bake muffins 18 minutes or the 8-inch pan for 20 to 25 minutes.

YIELD: 10 muffins or one 8-inch-square cornbread

CRANBERRY ALMOND MUFFINS

The flavour of lemon complements the cranberries and almonds.

1½ cups GEMS flour
½ cup brown sugar
2½ tsp baking powder
½ tsp baking soda
½ tsp guar gum
½ tsp salt
¼ cup vegetable oil

1 egg
½ cup unsweetened applesauce
½ cup milk
1 Tbsp lemon juice
2 tsp grated lemon zest
¾ cup dried cranberries
½ cup slivered almonds

1. Preheat oven to 350°F. Lightly grease muffin tin.
2. In mixing bowl blend GEMS flour, brown sugar, baking powder, baking soda, guar gum and salt. Make a well in the centre.
3. In separate bowl whisk together the oil, egg, applesauce, milk, lemon juice and zest.
4. Pour applesauce mixture into well and stir until dry ingredients are just moistened. Stir in cranberries and almonds.
5. Spoon ¼ cup batter into each muffin cup.
6. Bake about 20 minutes or until springy to touch. Place on rack to cool.

YIELD: 1 dozen

LEMON POPPY SEED MUFFINS

These delicately flavoured muffins turn out perfectly every time.

1 cup brown rice flour
¾ cup GEMS flour
⅓ cup granulated sugar
¼ cup poppy seeds
2 tsp baking powder
1 tsp baking soda
½ tsp guar gum
½ tsp salt
3 Tbsp vegetable oil

1 egg
½ tsp vanilla extract
1 cup plain yogurt
Juice and zest of 1 large lemon

NOTE
Poppy seeds quickly lose their flavour.
Store up to 6 months in the refrigerator.
Check for freshness before using.

1. Preheat oven to 350°F. Lightly grease muffin tin.
2. In mixing bowl blend brown rice flour, GEMS flour, sugar, poppy seeds, baking powder, baking soda, guar gum and salt. Make a well in the centre.
3. In separate bowl whisk the oil, egg, vanilla, yogurt, lemon juice and zest.
4. Pour yogurt mixture into centre of dry ingredients and stir until just moistened.
5. Spoon ¼ cup batter in each muffin cup.
6. Bake 16 to 18 minutes or until springy to touch. Place on rack to cool.

YIELD: 1 dozen

RHUBARB STREUSEL MUFFINS

The streusel topping makes these extra delicious.

1¼ cups GEMS flour
½ cup gluten-free quick oats
1 Tbsp baking powder
½ tsp baking soda
½ tsp salt
¼ tsp guar gum
¼ tsp ground cinnamon
¼ cup vegetable oil
1 egg
⅔ cup brown sugar

½ cup plain yogurt
1½ tsp cider vinegar
1 tsp vanilla extract
1½ cup diced fresh rhubarb

STREUSEL TOPPING
In a small bowl mix ¼ cup brown sugar, ¼ cup finely chopped walnuts, 2 Tbsp vegetable oil and ½ tsp cinnamon until blended.

1. Preheat oven to 350°F. Lightly grease muffin tin.
2. In mixing bowl blend GEMS flour, oats, baking powder, baking soda, salt, guar gum and cinnamon. Make a well in the centre.
3. In separate bowl whisk oil, egg, brown sugar, yogurt, vinegar and vanilla. Stir in the rhubarb.
4. Pour yogurt/rhubarb mixture into well and stir until dry ingredients are just moistened.
5. Spoon ¼ cup batter in each muffin cup. Sprinkle 1½ tsp streusel overtop of each muffin.
6. Bake for 20 minutes or until springy to touch. Place on rack to cool.

YIELD: 1 dozen

Pictured on page 56

BANANA BREAD

Enjoy this with a slice of mild-flavoured cheese.

1⅓ cups GEMS flour
⅓ cup chocolate chips
⅓ cup granulated sugar
1 Tbsp baking powder
½ tsp guar gum

½ tsp salt
1 cup mashed ripe banana (2 large)
⅔ cup milk
¼ cup vegetable oil

1. Preheat oven to 350°F. Lightly grease 8- × 4-inch loaf pan.
2. In mixing bowl combine GEMS flour, chocolate chips, sugar, baking powder, guar gum and salt.
3. In separate bowl blend the banana, milk and oil.
4. Pour wet mixture into centre of dry ingredients and lightly mix to blend.
5. Spoon batter into prepared pan. Bake until loaf is springy to touch or toothpick inserted in centre comes out clean, about 35 to 40 minutes.
6. Cool on rack 10 minutes before turning out of pan.

YIELD: 1 loaf

EGG FREE

DATE AND NUT BREAD

A long-time favourite that's always well received.

1¼ cups chopped dates
2½ tsp baking soda
2 Tbsp vegetable oil
¼ tsp salt
1¼ cups boiling water
1½ cups GEMS flour

½ tsp guar gum
1 beaten egg
⅓ cup plus 1 Tbsp granulated sugar
½ tsp grated lemon zest (optional)
½ cup chopped walnuts

1. In mixing bowl combine dates, baking soda, oil and salt. Stir in boiling water and let stand 20 minutes.
2. Preheat oven to 350°F. Lightly grease 9- × 5-inch loaf pan.
3. In small bowl beat egg, sugar and lemon zest (if using) and add to cooled date mixture.
4. Mix GEMS flour and guar gum and add to date mixture and lightly mix to blend. Fold in chopped nuts.
5. Spoon batter into prepared pan. Bake until loaf is springy to touch or toothpick inserted in centre comes out clean, about 35 to 40 minutes.
6. Cool on rack 10 minutes before turning out of pan.

YIELD: 1 loaf

DAIRY FREE

CRANBERRY NUT BREAD

The flavours of cranberries and orange mingle nicely.

1½ cups GEMS flour (reserve 1 Tbsp)
⅓ cup granulated sugar
2½ tsp baking powder
½ tsp guar gum
½ tsp baking soda
½ tsp salt

¼ cup firm butter
1 beaten egg
¾ cup orange juice
1 Tbsp orange zest
1 cup coarsely chopped dried cranberries
½ cup chopped walnuts

1. Preheat oven to 350°F. Lightly grease 8- × 4-inch loaf pan.
2. In mixing bowl combine GEMS flour, sugar, baking powder, guar gum, baking soda and salt.
3. With pastry blender cut butter into flour mixture.
4. Blend egg, orange juice and zest in small bowl. Mix reserved 1 Tbsp GEMS flour with cranberries and nuts.
5. Pour wet mixture into centre of dry ingredients and lightly mix to blend. Stir in cranberry mixture.
6. Spoon batter into prepared pan. Bake until loaf is springy to touch or toothpick inserted in centre comes out clean, 45 to 50 minutes.
7. Cool on rack 10 minutes before turning out of pan.

YIELD: 1 loaf

LEMON LOAF

The lemon glaze is the icing on the cake.

1¼ cup GEMS flour
2 tsp baking powder
½ tsp guar gum
¼ tsp salt
¼ cup softened butter
½ cup granulated sugar
1 beaten egg

1 Tbsp grated lemon zest
¼ cup milk

GLAZE
Mix 2 Tbsp granulated sugar with
  2 Tbsp lemon juice.

1. Preheat oven to 350°F. Lightly grease 8- × 4-inch loaf pan.
2. In mixing bowl combine GEMS flour, baking powder, guar gum and salt.
3. In separate bowl cream butter and sugar. Add egg and beat until blended. Stir in lemon zest and milk.
4. Pour wet mixture into centre of dry ingredients and mix lightly to blend.
5. Spoon batter into prepared pan. Bake until loaf is springy to touch or toothpick inserted in centre comes out clean, 30 to 35 minutes.
6. Remove from oven and, with a toothpick, poke small holes in the top of the loaf. Drizzle with glaze.
7. Cool completely before turning out of pan.

YIELD: 1 loaf

ORANGE KISS-ME LOAF

Make this once and you will be hooked—it's that good!

1 small orange, unpeeled, seeded and
   quartered
¾ cup raisins
1¾ cup GEMS flour (reserve ¼ cup)
2 tsp baking powder
1 tsp baking soda
¾ tsp guar gum
½ tsp salt
⅓ cup softened butter
⅔ cup granulated sugar
1 egg
¾ cup buttermilk

1. Preheat oven to 350°F. Lightly grease a 9- × 5-inch loaf pan.
2. Place quartered orange in food processor and pulse until chopped. Add raisins and pulse briefly.
3. In mixing bowl combine the 1½ cups GEMS flour, baking powder, baking soda, guar gum and salt.
4. In separate bowl cream butter and sugar. Add egg and beat until blended. Mix the reserved ¼ cup flour with orange/raisin mixture and add to egg mixture followed by buttermilk.
5. Pour wet mixture into centre of dry ingredients and lightly mix to blend.
6. Spoon batter into prepared pan and bake until loaf is springy to touch or toothpick inserted in centre comes out clean, about 40 to 45 minutes.
7. Cool on rack 10 minutes before turning out of pan.

YIELD: 1 loaf

PINEAPPLE ZUCCHINI LOAF

Leaving the skin on the zucchini adds colour and fibre.

1 cup GEMS flour
½ cup brown rice flour
2 tsp baking soda
1 tsp guar gum
½ tsp ground cinnamon
½ tsp salt
⅔ cup granulated sugar

⅓ cup vegetable oil
8 oz can unsweetened crushed pineapple, undrained
1 cup grated zucchini, lightly packed
1 tsp lemon juice

1. Preheat oven to 350°F. Lightly grease 8- × 4-inch loaf pan.
2. In mixing bowl combine GEMS flour, brown rice flour, baking soda, guar gum, cinnamon and salt.
3. In separate bowl beat the sugar and oil. Stir in crushed pineapple, zucchini and lemon juice.
4. Pour wet mixture into centre of dry ingredients and lightly mix to blend.
5. Spoon batter into prepared pan and bake until loaf is springy to touch or toothpick inserted in centre comes out clean, about 40 to 45 minutes.
6. Cool on rack 10 minutes before turning out of pan.

YIELD: 1 loaf

EGG & DAIRY FREE

SPICY PUMPKIN BREAD

Make this flavourful loaf your traditional autumn fare.

1½ cup GEMS flour
1 Tbsp baking powder
½ tsp baking soda
1½ tsp ground cinnamon
½ tsp ground ginger
½ tsp ground nutmeg
½ tsp guar gum
½ tsp salt

Pinch ground cloves
1 Tbsp ground flax plus 3 Tbsp hot water
⅓ cup vegetable oil
¼ cup brown sugar
¼ cup golden syrup
1 cup canned pumpkin
½ cup raisins
½ cup chopped walnuts

1. Preheat oven to 350°F. Lightly grease 9- × 5-inch loaf pan.
2. In mixing bowl combine GEMS flour, baking powder, baking soda, cinnamon, ginger, nutmeg, guar gum, salt and cloves.
3. In separate bowl combine flax/water mixture, oil, brown sugar and golden syrup and beat until blended. Stir in pumpkin.
4. Pour wet ingredients into centre of dry ingredients and mix lightly to blend. Fold in raisins and chopped nuts.
5. Spoon batter into prepared pan. Bake until loaf is springy to touch or toothpick inserted in centre comes out clean, about 50 minutes.
6. Cool on rack 10 minutes before turning out of pan.

YIELD: 1 loaf

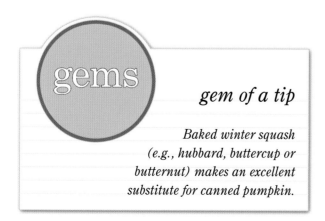

gems

gem of a tip

Baked winter squash (e.g., hubbard, buttercup or butternut) makes an excellent substitute for canned pumpkin.

EGG & DAIRY FREE

Pictured on page 58

STRAWBERRY AND RHUBARB LOAF

*The combination of strawberries, rhubarb
and lemon is scrumptious.*

1⅔ cups GEMS flour
½ cup granulated sugar
½ cup finely chopped walnuts
2 tsp baking soda
1 tsp guar gum
¼ tsp salt

¼ tsp ground nutmeg
⅓ cup vegetable oil
¾ cup sweetened stewed rhubarb
¾ cup mashed strawberries
2 tsp grated lemon zest

1. Preheat oven to 350°F. Lightly grease 9- × 5-inch loaf pan.
2. In mixing bowl combine GEMS flour, sugar, walnuts, baking soda, guar gum, salt and nutmeg.
3. In separate bowl whisk oil, rhubarb, strawberries and lemon zest.
4. Pour fruit mixture into centre of dry ingredients and lightly mix to blend.
5. Spoon batter into prepared pan. Bake until loaf is springy to touch or toothpick inserted in centre comes out clean, about 50 minutes.
6. Cool on rack 10 minutes before turning out of pan.

YIELD: 1 loaf

EGG & DAIRY FREE

FRESH CRANBERRY LOAF

The tang of the cranberries adds appeal.

1¾ cups GEMS flour
2 Tbsp ground flax or rice bran
2 tsp baking powder
½ tsp baking soda
½ tsp guar gum
⅔ cup brown sugar
⅓ cup butter, melted

2 eggs
1 cup orange juice
¾ cup chopped dried apricots
1 cup gluten-free cornflakes
1 cup cranberries (fresh or frozen,
 not thawed)

1. Preheat oven to 350°F. Lightly grease a 9- × 5-inch loaf pan.
2. In mixing bowl blend GEMS flour, bran or ground flax, baking powder, baking soda, guar gum, brown sugar and set aside.
3. In another bowl whisk together the butter, eggs and orange juice. Stir in the cornflakes and dried apricots and let stand 5 minutes.
4. Add cereal mixture to dry ingredients, stirring until just moistened.
5. Fold in cranberries, being careful not to overmix.
6. Spoon evenly in prepared pan and bake 45 to 50 minutes or until a tester inserted in centre comes out clean.

YIELD: 1 loaf

Hazelnut and Cranberry Biscotti, page 83

Cookies

Date Nut Drops, facing page

COOKIES

» Have all ingredients at room temperature.

» White sugar is best for crisp cookies. Brown sugar and honey absorb moisture from the air, causing the cookies to soften as they stand.

» Butter holds more moisture than shortening thus melts faster, producing a flat, thin and crisp cookie.

» Check cookies for doneness at the earliest time called for.

» Heavy, light-coloured pans bake cookies evenly and prevent browning too quickly. Pans that are lightweight and deep coloured tend to absorb more heat, bake quicker and over-brown.

» Placing cookie dough on a baking sheet that hasn't completely cooled can affect the texture and shape of the cookie.

» Transferring baked cookies to brown paper will absorb excess fat. Store crisp and soft cookies separately in airtight containers.

DATE NUT DROPS

These travel easily and are good keepers.

1 cup GEMS flour

1 tsp ground cinnamon

½ tsp baking soda

⅓ tsp salt

¼ tsp guar gum

⅓ cup soft butter

¼ cup brown sugar

¼ cup granulated sugar

1 egg

2 Tbsp milk

1 tsp vanilla extract

1¼ cups gluten-free quick oats

¾ cup chopped dates, lightly packed

1 cup walnuts, coarsely chopped

1. Preheat oven to 375°F. Lightly grease two baking sheets.
2. Combine GEMS flour, cinnamon, baking soda, salt and guar gum and set aside.
3. In mixing bowl cream butter and sugars. Add egg, milk and vanilla and beat until thoroughly blended. Add dry ingredients and mix to combine.
4. Stir in oats, dates and walnuts until well mixed.
5. Drop small spoonfuls of dough 1½ inches apart on prepared pan. Press lightly with fork.
6. Bake 10 to 12 minutes. Place on rack to cool.

YIELD: 3 dozen

Pictured opposite

SUGAR COOKIES

This dough will keep in the fridge for up to two weeks.

½ cup soft butter

⅔ cup icing sugar

1 egg

½ tsp vanilla extract

¼ tsp almond extract

1¼ cups brown rice flour

½ tsp baking soda

½ tsp cream of tartar

¼ tsp guar gum

Granulated sugar for sprinkling

1. In mixing bowl cream butter and icing sugar. Add egg and extracts and beat until thoroughly blended.
2. Add brown rice flour, baking soda, cream of tartar and guar gum to butter mixture and stir to combine.
3. Chill dough until firm enough to roll. Place on waxed paper and roll. Press into a square, rectangular or round log. Chill until firm.
4. Preheat oven to 375°F. Lightly grease two baking sheets.
5. Cut log into ⅛-inch slices and sprinkle each cookie with granulated sugar. Place 2 inches apart on baking sheet.
6. Bake 8 minutes. Let sit on pan 2 to 3 minutes. Place on rack to cool.

YIELD: 2 dozen

PAINTBRUSH COOKIES

Kids will find these great fun!

Prepare recipe for Sugar Cookies, facing page.

1. Mix 1 egg yolk with ½ tsp water.
2. Divide into very small portions.
3. Add one drop of food colouring to each portion.
4. Paint designs on cookies with small paintbrush.
5. Bake according to directions.

YIELD: 2 dozen

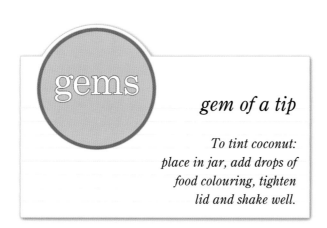

gems

gem of a tip

*To tint coconut:
place in jar, add drops of
food colouring, tighten
lid and shake well.*

ALMOND BISCOTTI

These cookies are baked twice to make them extra crisp.

2 cups almonds, unblanched (reserve ½ cup chopped)
2½ cups GEMS flour
1 Tbsp baking powder
½ tsp guar gum

½ tsp salt
½ tsp aniseed, finely crushed
½ cup soft butter
1¼ cups granulated sugar
1 egg and 2 egg whites

1. Preheat oven to 325°F. Have ungreased baking sheet ready.
2. Spread almonds evenly on baking sheet and toast 10 to 12 minutes. Cool.
3. In food processor coarsely chop toasted almonds and set aside ½ cup. Grind remaining nuts into flour. Add GEMS flour, baking powder, guar gum, salt and aniseed. Pulse to mix.
4. Add butter, sugar and beaten eggs and pulse until mixture begins to form a ball.
5. Turn dough onto lightly floured surface and knead in reserved almonds.
6. Divide dough into two balls, patting each ball into an oval-shaped log about 1½ inches in diameter. Score or mark each log diagonally. Lines should be ⅓ inch apart and ⅛ inch deep.
7. Place logs on an ungreased baking sheet and bake for 30 minutes. Remove logs from oven and cool for 20 minutes. Lower oven temperature to 200°F.
8. With a sharp knife carefully slice through markings and lay pieces on their sides. Bake 20 more minutes. Place on rack to cool.

YIELD: 2 dozen

HAZELNUT AND CRANBERRY BISCOTTI

Toasted hazelnuts give this cookie its wonderful flavour.

Prepare recipe for Almond Biscotti, facing page, with this variation:

1. Replace the 2 cups almonds with 1½ cups toasted hazelnuts and ½ cup chopped cranberries.
2. Grind the hazelnuts into the flour.
3. Use the cranberries to replace the chopped almonds.
4. Replace the aniseed with the juice and grated zest of one lemon.

YIELD: 2 dozen

Pictured on page 76

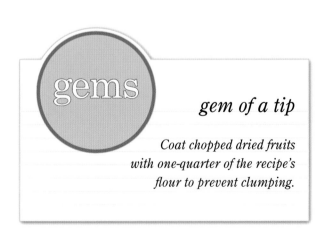

gems

gem of a tip

Coat chopped dried fruits with one-quarter of the recipe's flour to prevent clumping.

OATCAKES

Flat, crisp and not too sweet.

2½ cups gluten-free quick oats
½ tsp baking powder
2 Tbsp brown sugar
¼ tsp salt

3 Tbsp soft butter
5 to 6 Tbsp hot water
Extra quick oats for rolling

1. Preheat oven to 350°F. Have ungreased baking sheet ready.
2. In food processor pulse oats into flour. Add baking powder, sugar and salt and pulse to blend.
3. Melt butter in the hot water. Slowly pour into dry ingredients and pulse until dough begins to form a ball.
4. Sprinkle oats on waxed paper. Place dough on top of oats and pat into a small circle. Sprinkle oats overtop. Cover with waxed paper and roll into a large circle about ⅛ inch thick. Sprinkle top with fresh oats. Cut into wedges or cut out oatcakes with cookie cutter.
5. Bake 25 to 30 minutes. Place on rack to cool.

YIELD: 8 wedges or 12 oatcakes

EGG FREE

JEAN'S ALMOND MERINGUES

I got this original recipe from Jean, a member of my university women's group. It is prized to this day among her grandmother Mary Dawson Hicks's progeny.

3 egg whites, room temperature
½ tsp vinegar
Pinch salt

¾ cup granulated sugar
¼ tsp vanilla extract
⅔ cup whole unblanched almonds

1. Preheat oven to 150°F (not a typo; these really do bake at a low temperature!). Line two baking sheets with parchment paper.
2. Combine egg whites, vinegar and salt in small bowl of stand mixer and beat until soft peaks form.
3. Increase speed while slowly adding sugar, 1 Tbsp at a time, beating until egg whites are stiff and shiny and sugar has dissolved. Add vanilla.
4. Fold in almonds.
5. Drop by small teaspoonsful 1 inch apart on parchment-lined baking sheet.
6. Bake for approximately 4 hours. Turn oven off. Turn on oven light and leave meringues in oven another 4 hours or overnight. This will ensure the meringues dry out thoroughly and remain white.
7. Store in an airtight container.

YIELD: 3 dozen

DAIRY & FAT FREE

COCONUT MACAROONS

These are moist, chewy and good.

3 egg whites, room temperature
1 tsp vinegar
¼ tsp salt
⅔ cup granulated sugar

1 tsp vanilla extract
⅓ cup brown rice flour
2½ cups shredded, unsweetened coconut

1. Preheat oven to 325°F. Line one baking sheet with parchment paper.
2. Combine egg whites, vinegar and salt in small bowl of stand mixer and beat until soft peaks form.
3. Increasing the speed slowly, add sugar, 1 Tbsp at a time, beating until egg whites are stiff and shiny and sugar has dissolved. Add vanilla.
4. With a wire whisk fold brown rice flour into egg whites to blend. Stir in coconut.
5. Place small spoonfuls of mixture 2 inches apart on prepared pan.
6. Bake 20 minutes until golden brown and slightly soft to touch. Place on rack to cool.

YIELD: 2½ dozen

DAIRY FREE & FAT FREE

APPLE 'N' RAISIN COOKIES

These spicy-sweet cookies soften as they stand.

½ cup raisins (cover with ¼ cup boiling
   water and set aside to cool)
1½ cups GEMS flour
1 tsp baking soda
1 tsp ground cinnamon
¼ tsp salt
¼ tsp guar gum

⅛ tsp ground cloves
⅓ cup soft butter
⅔ cup brown sugar
1 egg
½ cup applesauce
½ tsp vanilla extract
½ cup chopped walnuts

1. Preheat oven to 375°F. Lightly grease two baking sheets.
2. Combine GEMS flour, baking soda, cinnamon, salt, guar gum and cloves and set aside.
3. In mixing bowl cream butter and sugar. Add egg and beat until thoroughly blended. Stir in applesauce and vanilla.
4. Add dry ingredients to wet ingredients and mix until blended. Stir in raisins (including liquid) and nuts.
5. Drop small spoonfuls of dough 1½ inches apart on prepared pan.
6. Bake 8 to 10 minutes or until nicely browned. Place on rack to cool.

YIELD: 2½ dozen

SOUR CREAM KISSES

The combination of sour cream and nutmeg is addictive.

1½ cups brown rice flour
1 tsp baking powder
½ tsp baking soda
½ tsp ground nutmeg
½ tsp guar gum

⅓ cup soft butter
½ cup granulated sugar
1 egg
½ cup sour cream
⅓ cup finely chopped walnuts

1. Preheat oven to 375°F. Lightly grease two baking sheets.
2. Combine brown rice flour, baking powder, baking soda, nutmeg and guar gum and set aside.
3. In mixing bowl cream butter and sugar. Add egg and beat until thoroughly blended. Add sour cream.
4. Blend flour mixture into wet ingredients. Stir in walnuts.
5. Drop small spoonfuls of dough 1 inch apart on prepared pan.
6. Bake 8 minutes. Place on rack to cool.

YIELD: 3 dozen

RAGGED ROBINS

*This was a real treat Mom made for me
when I was a little girl.*

2 egg whites, room temperature
¼ tsp cream of tartar
Pinch salt
¼ cup granulated sugar
½ tsp vanilla extract

1 cup dates coarsely chopped dates,
  not packed
⅓ cup coarsely chopped walnuts
½ cup glacé cherry halves
2 heaping cups gluten-free cornflakes

1. Preheat oven to 325°F. Lightly grease one baking sheet.
2. Combine egg whites, cream of tartar and salt in small bowl of stand mixer and beat until soft peaks form.
3. Increasing the speed slowly, add sugar, 1 Tbsp at a time, beating until egg whites are stiff and shiny and sugar has dissolved. Add vanilla last.
4. Combine dates, nuts and cherries and fold into egg whites. Fold in cornflakes last.
5. Drop tablespoonsful of mixture 2 inches apart on prepared pan.
6. Bake for 15 minutes. Place on rack to cool.

YIELD: 1½ dozen

DAIRY & FAT FREE

LEBKUCHEN

The recipe for these make-ahead cookies originated in Germany.

1¾ cups GEMS flour (reserve ⅓ cup)
¾ tsp baking soda
½ tsp guar gum
¼ tsp ground cinnamon
⅛ tsp each of ground nutmeg and salt
Pinch ground cloves
⅔ cup glacé fruitcake mix
⅓ cup slivered almonds
2 Tbsp glacé orange peel

½ tsp grated lemon zest
⅓ cup melted honey
¼ cup brown sugar
2 Tbsp water

LEMON GLAZE
Mix together ¼ cup icing sugar, ¼ tsp white
   corn syrup, 1 Tbsp lemon juice and ⅛ tsp
   lemon zest.

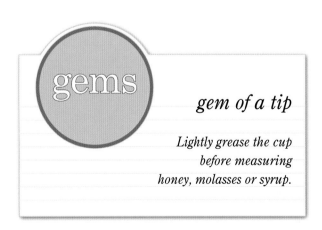

gems

gem of a tip

*Lightly grease the cup
before measuring
honey, molasses or syrup.*

1. In mixing bowl combine GEMS flour (less reserved ⅓ cup), baking soda, guar gum, cinnamon, nutmeg, salt and cloves and set aside.
2. In separate bowl combine the fruitcake mix, almonds, peel and lemon zest. Add reserved flour and toss to coat fruit.
3. Combine honey, brown sugar and water in saucepan and bring to a boil. Remove from heat to cool.
4. Add honey mixture to floured fruit mixture stirring until thoroughly mixed. The dough will be very stiff.
5. Wrap dough well with plastic wrap and place in cool area for 3 to 4 days.
6. Preheat oven to 350°F. Lightly grease two baking sheets.
7. Roll dough between two sheets of waxed paper in a rectangular shape, ¼ inch thick. Cut into 2- × 3-inch oblongs and place 1 inch apart on prepared pan.
8. Bake 10 to 12 minutes or until beginning to brown. Transfer to rack and spread glaze on the cookies as they cool.
9. These cookies can be eaten at any time; however, it is recommended that you store them in a sealed container between sheets of waxed paper to ripen for a period of 6 to 8 weeks. This time period will soften the cookie and enhance flavours.

YIELD: 2 dozen

EGG, DAIRY & FAT FREE

DOUBLE CHOCOLATE DROPS

A soft cake-like cookie appreciated by chocolate fans.

1 cup GEMS flour

¼ cup cocoa

1 tsp baking soda

¼ tsp guar gum

¼ cup granulated sugar

¼ cup brown sugar

¼ cup soft butter

1 egg

1 Tbsp corn syrup

1 tsp vanilla extract

½ cup chocolate chips

1. Preheat oven to 350°F. Lightly grease two baking sheets.
2. Combine GEMS flour, cocoa, baking soda and guar gum and set aside.
3. In mixing bowl cream sugars and butter. Add egg, corn syrup and vanilla and beat until thoroughly blended.
4. Add dry ingredients to wet ingredients and mix to blend. Stir in chocolate chips.
5. Drop small spoonfuls of batter 1½ inches apart on prepared pan. Flatten lightly with fork.
6. Bake for 8 to 10 minutes. Let sit 4 or 5 minutes before removing from pan. Place on rack to cool.

YIELD: 2½ dozen

DUTCH ALMOND SPICE COOKIES

These are similar to the traditional windmill-shaped cookies.

1¼ cups GEMS flour
⅓ cup ground almonds
1½ tsp ground cinnamon
½ tsp ground cloves
½ tsp ground nutmeg
½ baking powder

¼ tsp salt
¼ tsp guar gum
⅓ cup soft butter
⅔ cup brown sugar
2 Tbsp rum or ½ tsp rum flavouring or
   2 Tbsp water

1. Preheat oven to 325°F. Lightly grease one baking sheet.
2. Combine GEMS flour, ground almonds, cinnamon, cloves, nutmeg, baking powder, salt and guar gum.
3. In mixing bowl cream butter, sugar and rum. Add dry ingredients and stir to form soft dough.
4. Shape dough into a 2-inch-wide log and roll in waxed paper. Chill in refrigerator until firm. Cut into ¼-inch slices and place 2 inches apart on prepared pan.
5. Bake for 18 minutes. Place on rack to cool.

YIELD: 1½ dozen

EGG FREE

BEST-EVER DAD'S COOKIES

An old-fashioned cookie that is crisp and flavourful.

1 cup GEMS flour
1 cup gluten-free quick oats
1 tsp baking soda
¼ tsp salt
½ cup soft butter

⅔ cup brown sugar
1 egg
1 tsp vanilla extract
¾ cup unsweetened coconut

1. Preheat oven to 375°F. Lightly grease two baking sheets.
2. Combine GEMS flour, oats, baking soda and salt and set aside.
3. In mixing bowl cream butter and sugar. Add egg and vanilla and beat until thoroughly blended.
4. Add dry ingredients to creamed mixture blending until thoroughly mixed (the mixture will be stiff).
5. Add coconut and mix until thoroughly combined.
6. Roll into 1-inch balls and place 2 inches apart on baking pan. Press lightly with fork.
7. Bake 6 to 8 minutes. Place on rack to cool.

YIELD: 3 dozen

CRISPY GINGERSNAPS

Rolling a thinner dough makes for a crispier cookie.

1⅓ cups GEMS flour
1½ tsp ground cinnamon
½ tsp ground cloves
½ tsp ground ginger
1 tsp baking soda

⅓ cup soft butter
½ cup brown sugar
2 Tbsp water
½ Tbsp molasses
½ tsp lemon extract

1. Preheat oven to 350°F. Lightly grease one baking sheet.
2. Combine GEMS flour, cinnamon, cloves, ginger and baking soda and set aside.
3. In mixing bowl cream butter and sugar. Blend in water, molasses and lemon extract. Add dry ingredients to sugar mixture and mix until thoroughly blended.
4. Roll dough to ¼-inch thickness between two sheets of waxed paper (rolling a thinner dough makes for a crisper cookie). Cut out desired shapes with cookie cutter and place 1½ inches apart on baking pan.
5. Bake 8 minutes. Cool 5 minutes before removing from pan. Place on rack to cool.

YIELD: 2 dozen

EGG FREE

HAZELNUT MACAROONS

This is an Italian favourite.

1¼ cups hazelnuts
1 Tbsp plus 2 tsp GEMS flour
½ tsp ground cinnamon
⅛ tsp salt

2 egg whites
⅓ cup plus 1 Tbsp granulated sugar
Icing sugar for dusting

1. Preheat oven to 350°F. Line two baking sheets with parchment paper.
2. Finely grind hazelnuts in food processor. Add GEMS flour and cinnamon and set aside.
3. Combine salt and egg whites in small bowl of stand mixer and beat until soft peaks form.
4. Increase speed while slowly adding sugar, 1 Tbsp at a time, until egg whites are stiff and shiny and sugar is dissolved.
5. Fold hazelnut mixture into meringue until combined.
6. Drop heaping tablespoonsful of batter 1 inch apart on prepared pan.
7. Bake 16 to 18 minutes. Place on rack to cool.
8. Dust with a little icing sugar immediately before serving.

YIELD: 2½ dozen

DAIRY FREE & FAT FREE

JAM-JAMS

A soft, easy-to-prepare cookie kids will love to make.

1¼ cups brown rice flour
1½ tsp baking soda
½ tsp guar gum
⅓ cup soft butter

¼ cup brown sugar
1 egg
½ tsp vanilla extract
Jam or jelly

1. Preheat oven to 350°F. Lightly grease one baking sheet.
2. In small bowl combine brown rice flour, baking soda and guar gum. Set aside.
3. In mixing bowl cream butter and brown sugar. Add egg and beat until thoroughly blended. Stir in vanilla.
4. Drop spoonfuls of dough 1½ inches apart on baking pan.
5. Bake 8 minutes. Place on rack to cool.
6. Sandwich cookies with ½ tsp favourite jam or jelly.

YIELD: 1 dozen

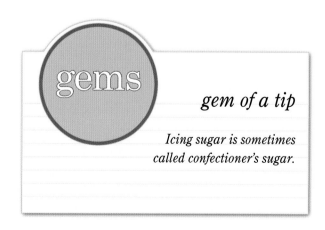

gems

gem of a tip

Icing sugar is sometimes called confectioner's sugar.

FOLK FESTIVAL SNACKS

These chewy, not-too-sweet cookies are full of grainy goodness.

¾ cup GEMS flour
⅔ cup gluten-free quick oats
½ tsp baking soda
½ tsp guar gum
½ tsp salt
3 Tbsp vegetable oil
⅓ cup brown sugar
¼ cup granulated sugar

¼ cup water
1 tsp vanilla extract
3 Tbsp ground flax
2 Tbsp coarsely ground sunflower seeds
½ cup dried cranberries (or chocolate chips, dairy free if required)
¼ cup unsweetened coconut

1. Preheat oven to 350°F. Lightly grease one baking sheet.
2. In small bowl combine GEMS flour, oats, baking soda, guar gum and salt and set aside.
3. In mixing bowl blend oil, sugars, water and vanilla.
4. Add flour mix to wet ingredients and stir until blended.
5. Stir in flax, sunflower seeds, cranberries or chocolate chips and coconut until thoroughly combined.
6. Drop spoonfuls of dough 2 inches apart on prepared pan. Press lightly with fork.
7. Bake 10 to 12 minutes. Place on rack to cool.

YIELD: 2 dozen

EGG & DAIRY FREE

ALMOND JAM SLICES

This Austrian marzipan-like treat is thanks to my friend Jette.

2 cups ground almonds

⅓ cup granulated sugar

1 egg white

¼ tsp almond extract

⅛ tsp salt

½ cup apricot jam

Icing sugar for work surface

1. Preheat oven to 350°F. Grease two large baking sheets.
2. In mixing bowl combine all ingredients except jam. Mixture should form a paste.
3. Sprinkle work surface with icing sugar.
4. Divide dough into four equal parts. Using your palms roll each piece into an 11-inch rope. Place two ropes on each baking sheet.
5. Using the side of your little finger press a groove down the centre of each rope leaving ¼ inch at each end.
6. Bake 10 minutes. Remove from oven. Spoon jam into grooves and return to oven for 10 minutes or until golden brown. Cool on rack.
7. Cut into 1-inch diagonal slices. Store in an airtight container for 1 week or freeze.

YIELD: 3½ dozen

DAIRY & FAT FREE

WHIPPED SHORTBREAD

Chilling the dough prevents cookies from spreading while baking.

1 cup extra-fine brown rice flour

½ cup tapioca starch

⅓ cup icing sugar

Pinch salt

½ cup soft butter

¼ tsp almond extract or ½ tsp vanilla
   extract

Glacé cherries, quartered (optional)

1. Preheat oven to 300° F. Have one ungreased baking sheet ready.
2. In mixing bowl combine dry ingredients with butter and extract. Beat mixture on low speed of mixer until it begins to form a ball. Chill 30 minutes.
3. Roll into walnut-sized balls and place 1 inch apart on baking pan or pat out into a ¼-inch-thick circle and use a cookie cutter to cut out desired shapes.
4. If desired, decorate tops with cherry quarters or mark criss-crosses with the tines of a fork.
5. Bake 18 to 20 minutes. Place on rack to cool.

YIELD: 1½ dozen

EGG FREE

PEANUT BUTTER AND ALMOND TREATS

These are delicious!

⅞ cup GEMS flour

2 Tbsp rice bran or ground flax

1 tsp baking soda

½ tsp guar gum

Pinch salt

¼ cup soft butter

⅔ cup smooth peanut butter

⅓ cup white sugar

⅓ cup brown sugar

3 Tbsp water

1 tsp vanilla extract

½ cup chopped slivered almonds

1. Preheat oven to 350°F. Lightly grease two baking sheets.
2. Combine GEMS flour, rice bran or flax, baking soda, guar gum and salt and set aside.
3. In mixing bowl cream butter and peanut butter. Blend in sugars, water and vanilla.
4. Add dry ingredients to butter/sugar mixture and mix to thoroughly combine. Add almonds.
5. Drop by rounded teaspoons 1½ inches apart on prepared pan. Press lightly with fork.
6. Bake 10 to 12 minutes. Place on rack to cool.

YIELD: 1½ dozen

EGG FREE

TRIPLE GINGER COOKIES

Gingery and chewy!

2 cups GEMS flour
1½ tsp ground ginger
1½ tsp baking soda
1 tsp ground cinnamon
½ tsp guar gum
¼ tsp salt
½ cup soft butter

⅔ cup brown sugar
1 egg
¼ cup molasses
1½ tsp finely grated fresh ginger
½ tsp vanilla extract
⅓ cup chopped crystallized ginger
Granulated sugar for rolling

1. Preheat oven to 325°F. Lightly grease two baking sheets.
2. Combine GEMS flour, ground ginger, baking soda, cinnamon, guar gum and salt and stir to blend. Set aside.
3. In mixing bowl cream butter and sugar. Add egg, molasses, fresh ginger and vanilla and beat until blended.
4. Add dry ingredients and mix well. Stir in crystallized ginger.
5. Shape dough into 1-inch balls, roll in granulated sugar and place 2 inches apart on baking sheet.
6. Bake 12 to 15 minutes. Place on rack to cool.

YIELD: 2½ dozen

LEMON WAFERS

Crunchy and lemony.

1¼ cups GEMS flour

⅓ cup cornmeal

Pinch salt

⅓ cup soft butter

½ cup granulated sugar

1 egg

1 Tbsp grated lemon zest

1. Preheat oven to 325°F. Lightly grease one baking sheet.
2. Combine GEMS flour, cornmeal and salt and set aside.
3. In mixing bowl cream butter and sugar. Add egg and lemon zest and beat until blended.
4. Combine dry ingredients with sugar mixture and mix thoroughly.
5. Drop by rounded teaspoons 1½ inch apart on prepared pan and lightly press with fork.
6. Bake 15 to 18 minutes. Place on rack to cool.

YIELD: 2 dozen

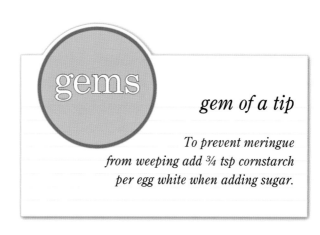

gems

gem of a tip

To prevent meringue from weeping add ¾ tsp cornstarch per egg white when adding sugar.

Scottish Shortbread, page 115

Squares & Bars

Coconut Raspberry Bars, page 110

SQUARES AND BARS

» Heavy shiny pans bake evenly and prevent browning too quickly.

» Cut your bars or squares after they are completely cooled.

» Squares and bars are convenient. They are quick to make, transport easily and can be cut into any size you desire.

» Many baked squares and bars are better kept in the pans in which they were baked. Be sure to keep them tightly covered.

» To freeze, separate layers with waxed paper and store well sealed for up to 3 months.

DAINTY ORANGE SQUARES

These moist and delicious cake-like squares are easy and quick to make.

⅓ cup butter

⅔ cup brown sugar

½ cup unsweetened applesauce

1 egg

1¼ tsp freshly grated orange zest

½ tsp vanilla extract

1 cup plus 2 Tbsp GEMS flour

2 tsp baking powder

½ tsp baking soda

½ tsp guar gum

¼ tsp salt

½ cup finely chopped walnuts

GLAZE

Beat together 1½ cups icing sugar, 2½ Tbsp fresh orange juice, ½ tsp vanilla extract and ¼ tsp freshly grated orange zest.

1. Preheat oven to 350° F. Lightly grease 9- × 13-inch pan.
2. In saucepan melt butter over low heat. Remove from heat and whisk in sugar, applesauce, egg, orange zest and vanilla.
3. Blend GEMS flour, baking powder, baking soda, guar gum and salt. Add to saucepan and beat until smooth. Stir in walnuts.
4. Spread mixture evenly into prepared pan. Bake 20 to 23 minutes.
5. Cool 15 minutes then ice with glaze.

YIELD: 24 bars

APRICOT SQUARES

These have a shortbread cookie base and a delightful apricot filling.

1 cup dried apricots
1 cup GEMS flour
¼ cup granulated sugar
½ tsp guar gum
¼ cup butter
1 egg
¾ cup brown sugar

2 Tbsp water
½ tsp vanilla extract
3 Tbsp GEMS flour
½ tsp baking powder
¼ tsp salt
½ cup chopped walnuts
½ cup unsweetened shredded coconut

1. In a small saucepan combine apricots with just enough water to cover and simmer until apricots are soft. Drain, cool and chop.
2. Preheat oven to 350°F. Lightly grease 8- × 8-inch pan.
3. In mixing bowl combine the 1 cup GEMS flour, sugar and guar gum. With pastry blender cut in butter until mixture is crumbly. Press into prepared pan and bake 10 minutes.
4. Using same bowl combine egg, brown sugar, water, vanilla, the 3 Tbsp GEMS flour, baking powder, salt and beat until blended. Stir in apricots, walnuts and coconut.
5. Spread mixture evenly over baked base. Bake an additional 25 minutes.
6. Cool before cutting into squares.

YIELD: 12 large squares

BUTTER TART SQUARES

These are as good as the tarts.

1 cup GEMS flour
½ cup brown rice flour
1 Tbsp icing sugar
½ tsp guar gum
⅓ cup butter
2 Tbsp water

⅔ cup brown sugar
2 Tbsp melted butter
1 egg
1 tsp vinegar
1 tsp vanilla extract
1 cup sultana raisins

1. Preheat oven to 350°F. Lightly grease 9- × 9-inch pan.
2. In mixing bowl combine GEMS flour, brown rice flour, icing sugar and guar gum. With pastry blender cut in butter and work mixture until crumbly. Add water to form a pastry.
3. Press mixture firmly into prepared pan. Bake 10 minutes.
4. Using same bowl stir together brown sugar, melted butter, egg, vinegar and vanilla and beat by hand until blended. Stir in raisins.
5. Spread mixture evenly over baked base. Bake an additional 25 minutes.
6. Cool completely before cutting.

YIELD: 25 small squares

COCONUT RASPBERRY BARS

*Elegant picnic fare—prepare a day ahead
and pack in sealed container.*

1½ cups brown rice flour
½ tsp baking powder
1 tsp guar gum
¼ tsp salt
⅓ cup butter
1 egg
2 Tbsp water

½ cup raspberry jam
3 Tbsp melted butter
⅔ cup granulated sugar
2 egg whites
1 tsp vanilla extract
2 cups unsweetened shredded coconut

1. Preheat oven to 325°F. Lightly grease 8- × 8-inch pan.
2. In mixing bowl combine brown rice flour, baking power, guar gum and salt.
   With pastry blender cut in butter until mixture is crumbly. Add egg and water
   and stir to combine.
3. Press mixture firmly into prepared pan. Bake 10 minutes.
4. Spread raspberry jam over baked shortbread base.
5. Using same mixing bowl combine melted butter, sugar, egg whites and
   vanilla and beat until fluffy. Stir in coconut to blend. Spread mixture over
   raspberry layer.
6. Bake 20 minutes, covering top if necessary to prevent over-browning.
7. Cool completely before cutting.

YIELD: 18 bars

Pictured on page 106

DATE SQUARES (MATRIMONIAL CAKE)

Soften dates briefly in microwave if necessary.

1½ cups chopped dates
¾ cup water
1½ Tbsp lemon juice
¼ tsp grated lemon zest
1 cup GEMS flour
1 tsp baking powder

½ tsp baking soda
½ tsp guar gum
¼ tsp salt
1 cup brown sugar
⅔ cup butter
2 cups gluten-free quick oats

1. In small saucepan combine dates, water, lemon juice and zest and cook over medium-low heat until blended. Cool completely.
2. Heat oven to 325°F. Lightly grease 9- × 9-inch pan.
3. In mixing bowl combine GEMS flour, baking powder, baking soda, guar gum, salt and brown sugar. With pastry blender cut in butter until mixture is crumbly. Mix in the oats.
4. Press 2½ cups of the oat mixture firmly into bottom of prepared pan. Spread date mixture evenly over this base.
5. Lightly press the remaining oat mixture overtop. Bake 45 to 50 minutes.
6. Cool completely before cutting.

YIELD: 16 large squares

EGG FREE

CHOCOLATE FUDGE BROWNIES

*Chocolate lovers will be in heaven when they
taste these delicious treats.*

1 cup GEMS flour
⅓ cup cocoa
1½ tsp baking powder
⅔ cup granulated sugar
¾ tsp salt
½ cup dairy-free chocolate chips, ground
½ tsp guar gum

½ cup water
1 Tbsp cornstarch
⅓ cup vegetable oil
3 Tbsp maple syrup
1 tsp vanilla extract
⅓ cup chopped walnuts or
    chopped dried sour cherries

1. Preheat oven to 350°F. Lightly grease 8- × 8-inch pan.
2. In mixing bowl combine GEMS flour, cocoa, baking powder, sugar, salt,
    ground chocolate chips and guar gum.
3. In separate bowl combine water and cornstarch. Add oil, maple syrup and
    vanilla and mix to blend.
4. Add wet ingredients to dry ingredients and beat until blended. Stir in
    walnuts or dried cherries.
5. Spread mixture evenly into pan. Bake 30 to 35 minutes.
6. Cool completely before cutting.

YIELD: 20 small squares

EGG & DAIRY FREE

gems

gem of a tip

*Natural cocoa is acidic.
Dutch processed cocoa, which
is darker and considered superior,
is neutral. Use either for general baking.*

LUSCIOUS LEMON SQUARES

Everyone's favourite!

1¼ cups brown rice flour
¼ cup icing sugar
½ tsp guar gum
¼ cup butter
1 egg

½ cup granulated sugar
2½ Tbsp fresh lemon juice
2 Tbsp brown rice flour
½ tsp baking powder
Zest of 1 large lemon

1. Preheat oven to 350°F. Lightly grease 8- × 8-inch pan.
2. In mixing bowl combine the 1¼ cups brown rice flour, icing sugar and guar gum. With pastry blender cut in butter until crumbly. Press evenly into prepared pan and bake 10 minutes.
3. Lower oven temperature to 325°F.
4. Using same bowl beat egg, sugar and lemon juice together. Add the 2 Tbsp brown rice flour, baking powder and lemon zest, mixing thoroughly.
5. Pour mixture over shortbread base and bake 15 minutes.
6. Cool completely before cutting. Sprinkle with a little icing sugar just prior to serving.

YIELD: 12 large squares

MAPLE PECAN SHORTBREAD

This is quickly made up in the food processor.

1 cup pecans

1 cup gluten-free quick oats

1 cup GEMS flour

¼ cup brown sugar

½ tsp baking powder

½ tsp guar gum

¼ tsp salt

¼ tsp ground cinnamon

⅓ cup soft butter

2 tsp vanilla extract

½ tsp almond extract

¼ cup maple syrup

1. Preheat oven to 300°F. Lightly grease 9- × 9-inch pan.
2. Place pecans in food processor and pulse to coarsely chop. Set aside ¼ cup.
3. Add oats to food processor and process until finely ground. Add the GEMS flour, brown sugar, baking powder, guar gum, salt and cinnamon and pulse to mix.
4. Add butter, vanilla and almond extract and pulse to mix. Continuing to pulse slowly, add maple syrup to form a soft ball.
5. Add reserved nuts and work with fingers to combine.
6. Press mixture into prepared pan and bake 30 minutes. Cover if necessary, as the fat content in the nuts may cause over-browning.
7. Cool completely before cutting.

YIELD: 24 bars

EGG FREE

SCOTTISH SHORTBREAD

This gluten-free version is as delicious as the real thing!

1¼ cups finely ground brown rice flour
¼ cup corn flour (not cornstarch)
½ cup butter

⅓ cup brown sugar
¼ tsp salt

1. Preheat oven to 300°F. Have ungreased 8- × 8-inch pan ready.
2. In food processor combine brown rice flour, corn flour, butter, brown sugar and salt. Pulse until mixture is crumbly.
3. Press firmly into ungreased pan.
4. There is less chance of breakage when you score the shortbread before it is baked. Score shortbread ⅛ inch deep, six rows across and three rows down.
5. Using the tip of fork tines poke three evenly spaced indentations in each rectangle. Bake 25 minutes.
6. Cool completely before cutting.

YIELD: 18 bars

EGG FREE

Pictured on page 104

PISTACHIO CARDAMOM SQUARES

This shortbread-like cookie comes from Iran.

1 cup butter
2 cups chickpea flour
1 cup icing sugar

1½ tsp ground cardamom
½ cup coarsely chopped pistachios

1. Preheat oven to 300°F. Have ungreased 9- × 9-inch pan ready.
2. Melt butter in a frying pan over low heat. Add chickpea flour in small amounts, stirring constantly with a wire whisk. Remove from heat. Cool slightly.
3. Stir in icing sugar and cardamom.
4. Pat dough into prepared pan.
5. Sprinkle chopped pistachios overtop, pressing them lightly into the dough. Bake 25 minutes.
6. Cool completely before cutting.

YIELD: 25 small squares

EGG FREE

GRANOLA BARS

Appease hunger pangs with these hearty bars.

1½ cups gluten-free quick oats
1¼ cups GEMS flour
2 tsp baking powder
½ tsp ground cinnamon
½ tsp ground allspice
¼ tsp ground ginger
1 tsp salt
¾ cup finely chopped apricots
½ cup chopped dried cranberries

½ cup sunflower seeds
¼ cup shredded unsweetened coconut
   or dairy-free chocolate chips
¾ cup unsweetened applesauce
½ cup apple juice
⅓ cup melted honey
2 Tbsp ground flax mixed with
   6 Tbsp hot water

1. Preheat oven to 400°F. Line 9- × 13-inch pan with parchment paper.
2. In large mixing bowl combine oats, GEMS flour, baking powder, cinnamon, allspice, ginger and salt. Stir in apricots, cranberries, sunflower seeds and coconut (or chocolate chips). Set aside.
3. In small bowl blend applesauce, apple juice, honey and flax/water mixture.
4. Pour wet mixture into dry ingredients and stir to mix.
5. Spread into prepared pan. Bake about 20 minutes until lightly browned.

YIELD: 16 large bars

EGG, DAIRY & FAT FREE

Angel Food Cake, page 125

Cakes & Cupcakes

Glazed Chocolate Cake Doughnuts, page 142
Old-Fashioned Cake Doughnuts, page 141

CAKES AND CUPCAKES

» Have ingredients at room temperature.

» The correct size of pan is important, as it affects baking time.

» For best results it is preferable to make two separate cakes rather than doubling the recipe.

» Two cups of flour yield 1 dozen large cupcakes.

» For a delicately textured cake it is important to cream the butter and sugar thoroughly. Follow with the egg and beat until mixture is light and fluffy.

» To remove air bubbles from batter, grasp sides of pan, lift a few inches above counter and let drop. Repeat if necessary.

» A cake is baked if the top springs back when lightly pressed with fingertips or a toothpick inserted in the centre comes out clean.

FAVOURITE APPLE CAKE

Leave peel on apple for additional fibre.

1½ cups GEMS flour
1 Tbsp baking powder
½ tsp baking soda
1 tsp ground cinnamon
½ tsp salt
½ tsp guar gum

¼ cup soft butter
⅔ cup granulated sugar
1 tsp vanilla extract
¾ cup plain yogurt
1½ cups finely chopped apple

1. Preheat oven to 350°F. Line bottom of 8- × 8-inch pan with parchment paper and lightly grease sides.
2. Blend GEMS flour, baking powder, baking soda, cinnamon, salt and guar gum and set aside.
3. In mixing bowl cream butter, sugar and vanilla and beat until light and fluffy.
4. Add dry ingredients alternately with yogurt and beat until smooth.
5. Fold in chopped apple and spoon into prepared pan.
6. Bake 30 to 35 minutes. Place on rack to cool.

YIELD: One 8- × 8-inch cake

EGG FREE

SOUR CREAM SPICE CAKE WITH BROWN SUGAR FROSTING

A nice variation is to replace 3 Tbsp of the GEMS flour with 3 Tbsp cocoa.

1½ cups GEMS flour
1 tsp baking soda
1 tsp ground cinnamon
½ tsp ground ginger
½ tsp guar gum
½ tsp salt
¼ tsp ground nutmeg
⅛ tsp ground cloves
⅓ cup soft butter
½ cup brown sugar

1 egg
1 cup light sour cream

BROWN SUGAR FROSTING
In small saucepan melt ¼ cup butter. Add ⅓ cup light cream and 1¼ cups brown sugar. Bring to a boil for 1 minute. Remove from heat and blend in 1½ cups icing sugar for desired consistency.

1. Preheat oven to 350°F. Lightly grease bottom of 8- × 8-inch pan.
2. Blend GEMS flour, baking soda, cinnamon, ginger, guar gum, salt, nutmeg and cloves and set aside.
3. In mixing bowl cream butter and brown sugar until blended. Add egg and beat until light and fluffy.
4. Add dry ingredients to creamed mixture alternately with sour cream and beat until blended. Spoon into prepared pan.
5. Bake about 30 to 35 minutes. Place on rack to cool.

YIELD: One 8- × 8-inch cake

BOILED RAISIN CAKE

Tasty, moist and inexpensive.

Prepare recipe for Sour Cream Cake, facing page, with this variation:

1. In saucepan combine 1 cup sultana raisins and 1½ cups water. Boil for 4 to
    5 minutes. Cool and drain, reserving liquid.
2. Replace sour cream with reserved liquid.
3. Fold in the raisins. Bake as above.

YIELD: One 8- × 8-inch cake

CHOCOLATE ZUCCHINI CAKE WITH CHOCOLATE FROSTING

This is easy to prepare, remains moist and freezes well.

1½ cups GEMS flour
3 Tbsp cocoa
1 tsp baking soda
½ tsp guar gum
¼ tsp salt
¼ cup canola oil
⅔ cup granulated sugar
1 egg
¼ tsp instant coffee powder dissolved in
    1 tsp vanilla
½ cup buttermilk

1 cup grated zucchini, drained and lightly
    packed
½ cup chocolate chips (optional)

CHOCOLATE FROSTING
Cream 3 Tbsp soft butter, ½ tsp vanilla extract, dash salt and 2 cups icing sugar with 2 to 2½ Tbsp milk. Melt 2 squares unsweetened chocolate and add to mixture. Blend until creamy smooth and the right consistency for spreading.

1. Preheat oven to 350°F. Lightly grease bottom of an 8- × 8-inch pan.
2. In small bowl blend GEMS flour, cocoa, baking soda, guar gum and salt.
3. In mixing bowl combine oil, sugar, egg, coffee/vanilla mixture and buttermilk and beat until blended.
4. Combine flour mixture with liquid ingredients and beat until thoroughly mixed.
5. Stir in zucchini and chocolate chips (if using) and spoon into prepared pan.
6. Bake 25 minutes. Place on rack to cool.

YIELD: One 8- × 8-inch cake

ANGEL FOOD CAKE

Small cartons of liquid egg whites are available in the dairy section. Note that angel food cake cannot rise if baked in a pan with a non-stick surface.

1½ cups egg whites, room temperature

1½ tsp cream of tartar

1 cup granulated sugar

½ tsp salt

1 tsp almond extract

1 tsp vanilla extract

3 Tbsp tapioca starch mixed with
  2 Tbsp icing sugar

¾ cup brown rice flour

1. Preheat oven to 375°F. Place oven rack on bottom rung. Have an ungreased aluminum 10-inch tube pan ready (not non-stick).
2. Place egg whites in large bowl of stand mixer and beat until foamy. Add cream of tartar and beat until soft peaks form.
3. Increase speed to high. Slowly add sugar 2 Tbsp at a time, beating until peaks are stiff and shiny, about 10 minutes. Add salt and extracts at the end.
4. Check to make sure the sugar granules have dissolved by rubbing a little of the meringue between thumb and index finger.
5. Reduce speed to low. Add the tapioca starch/icing sugar mixture just to blend. Remove beaters.
6. Using a sieve, sprinkle one-third of the brown rice flour over the egg whites, folding it in with a rolling motion of a large metal whisk.
7. Spoon batter into pan. With a knife cut through the batter in a circular motion to remove air bubbles.
8. Bake for 20 minutes then lower oven temperature to 300°F and bake a further 20 to 25 minutes. Invert to cool.

YIELD: One 10-inch tube cake

DAIRY & FAT FREE

Pictured on page 118

HOT MILK SPONGE CAKE

Use for a jelly roll, English trifle, tiramisu or Boston cream pie!

1¼ cups brown rice flour
2 tsp baking powder
½ tsp salt
¼ tsp guar gum

3 large eggs
¾ cup granulated sugar
1 tsp vanilla extract
½ cup less 1 tsp milk

1. Preheat oven to 325° F. Lightly grease a 9- × 9-inch pan or line a 15- × 10- × 1-inch jelly roll pan with parchment paper.
2. In a small bowl blend the brown rice flour, baking powder, salt and guar gum and set aside.
3. In stand mixer, beat eggs, sugar and vanilla together on high speed until very thick, about 5 minutes. While eggs are beating, heat the milk until just simmering.
4. Slowly pour the hot milk into the egg mixture in a steady stream as you continue beating on high.
5. With a wire whisk gently fold dry ingredients into egg mixture until evenly combined.
6. Pour into square pan and bake until golden brown, 20 to 25 minutes. For jelly roll spread batter evenly over pan and bake 13 to 15 minutes.
7. Cool in pan 15 minutes then invert the cake onto rack to finish cooling.
8. For jelly roll, loosen edges around cake and trim sides. Immediately turn upside-down on a tea towel sprinkled with icing sugar. While hot, roll cake and towel from narrow end. Cool on wire rack. Unroll cake, remove towel and spread with jam or filling and reroll.

YIELD: One 9- × 9-inch cake or 15-inch jelly roll

FAT FREE

DREAM CAKE

A delicately textured white cake.

1 cup brown rice flour
½ cup quinoa flour
1 Tbsp baking powder
¼ tsp salt
½ tsp guar gum
¼ cup soft butter

½ cup granulated sugar
2 egg whites
1 tsp vanilla extract
½ tsp almond extract
⅔ cup milk

1. Preheat oven to 350°F. Lightly grease bottom of 8- × 8-inch pan.
2. Blend brown rice flour, quinoa flour, baking powder, salt and guar gum, and set aside.
3. In mixing bowl cream butter and sugar. Add egg whites and extracts and beat until light and fluffy.
4. Add dry ingredients to sugar mixture alternately with the milk, beginning and ending with the dry ingredients and beat until smooth. Spoon into prepared pan.
5. Bake 20 to 25 minutes. Place on rack to cool.

YIELD: One 8- × 8-inch cake

MARBLE CAKE

This cake has pizzazz!

Prepare recipe for Dream Cake, previous page, with this variation:

1. Omit the almond extract.
2. Pour two-thirds of the batter into cake pan. To remaining batter, add 1 square melted unsweetened chocolate mixed with ¼ tsp baking soda dissolved in 1½ Tbsp boiling water.
3. Drop 3 Tbsp amounts of chocolate batter here and there into the white cake batter.
4. Cut through batter two or three times with a knife for marble effect.
5. Bake as directed for Dream Cake.

YIELD: One 8- × 8-inch cake

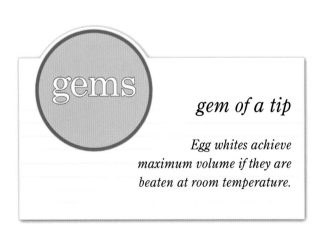

gems

gem of a tip

Egg whites achieve maximum volume if they are beaten at room temperature.

COFFEE CAKE

Tasty as is, and more so when served warm.

1½ cups brown rice flour
2 tsp baking powder
1 tsp baking soda
½ tsp guar gum
¼ tsp salt
⅓ cup soft butter
⅓ cup granulated sugar
1 egg

½ tsp vanilla extract
1⅓ cups plain yogurt

FILLING
Mix together ½ cup brown sugar,
    1½ tsp ground cinnamon and ½ cup
    coarsely chopped walnuts.

1. Preheat oven to 300°F. Grease bottom of 8- × 8-inch pan.
2. In small bowl blend brown rice flour, baking powder, baking soda, guar gum and salt and set aside.
3. In mixing bowl cream butter and sugar until blended. Add egg and vanilla and beat until light and fluffy.
4. Add dry ingredients to butter mixture alternately with the yogurt until mixture is blended, beginning and ending with the dry ingredients.
5. Spoon half the batter into prepared pan. Sprinkle filling overtop. Cover evenly with remaining batter.
6. Bake 40 to 45 minutes. Place on rack to cool.

YIELD: One 8- × 8-inch cake

PANFORTE

This thin and rich Italian fruitcake is distinguished by its spices.

½ cup GEMS flour
2 Tbsp cocoa
1 tsp ground cinnamon
¼ tsp ground coriander
¼ tsp ground nutmeg
⅛ tsp ground cloves
¼ tsp guar gum
⅛ tsp salt

Pinch ground white pepper
1¼ cups coarsely chopped dried figs
1 cup coarsely chopped walnuts
½ cup coarsely chopped blanched almonds
½ cup coarsely chopped glacé orange peel
½ cup coarsely chopped glacé citron
⅔ cup granulated sugar
⅔ cup light corn syrup

1. Preheat oven to 300°F. Lightly grease the bottom and sides of a 9-inch spring form pan. Cut circle of parchment paper and place on bottom of greased pan.
2. In small bowl blend GEMS flour, cocoa, cinnamon, coriander, nutmeg, cloves, guar gum, salt and white pepper and set aside.
3. In a large bowl, combine the figs, walnuts, almonds, peel and citron. Add dry ingredients and stir to mix.
4. In small saucepan, combine the sugar and corn syrup and cook over medium-low heat until syrup forms firm ball when dropped into cold water or reaches 245°F on candy thermometer.
5. Immediately pour the syrup into the fruit/nut/flour mixture, stirring quickly until flour is thoroughly moistened.
6. Spoon the batter into prepared pan and press evenly with back of greased spatula.
7. Bake 45 minutes. Set on rack and cool completely in pan.
8. Invert on a plate lined with waxed paper. Peel off parchment paper. Turn cake right side up and sprinkle with icing sugar.

YIELD: 12 wedges

EGG, DAIRY & FAT FREE

PRIZE-WINNING CARROT CAKE WITH CREAM CHEESE FROSTING

This cake is perfection!

1¼ cups GEMS flour
2 tsp baking powder
¼ tsp baking soda
1½ tsp ground cinnamon
½ tsp salt
¼ tsp guar gum
⅓ cup vegetable oil
⅔ cup granulated sugar
2 egg whites
1 tsp vanilla extract
2½ tsp lemon juice

1 cup crushed pineapple with juice
1½ cups grated carrot, lightly packed
½ cup raisins, chopped
⅓ cup chopped walnuts
⅓ cup unsweetened shredded coconut

CREAM CHEESE FROSTING

Cream 1 cup soft light cream cheese and 3 Tbsp soft butter until blended. Blend in ½ cup icing sugar and spread over cooled cake. Refrigerate.

1. Preheat oven to 350°F. Prepare 9- × 9-inch pan and line bottom with parchment paper.
2. Blend GEMS flour, baking powder, baking soda, cinnamon, salt and guar gum and set aside.
3. In mixing bowl beat together oil and sugar. Add egg whites, vanilla and lemon juice and beat until blended.
4. Blend in dry ingredients alternately with crushed pineapple.
5. Add in carrot, raisins, walnuts and coconut and mix until thoroughly blended.
6. Pour into pan and bake 25 to 30 minutes. Place on rack to cool.

YIELD: One 9- × 9-inch cake

RICH DARK FRUITCAKE

Read through entire recipe before commencing.

FRUIT AND NUT MIXTURE

In a very large bowl or roasting pan
combine the following fruit and nuts.
Marinate fruit/nut mixture for one week.
Stir daily.

4 cups sultana raisins
1¼ cups currants
3 cups chopped dates
1 cup glacé cherries cut in half
1 cup chopped mixed peel
2 Tbsp chopped crystallized ginger
1 small peeled apple, finely chopped
1½ cups sliced almonds
1 cup chopped walnuts or pecans
½ cup chopped dried apricots
½ cup chopped figs (optional)
2½ cups red wine

BATTER

1½ cups GEMS flour
1 tsp baking soda
1 tsp ground cinnamon
½ tsp guar gum
Pinch ground cloves
1 cup soft butter
⅔ cup brown sugar
4 egg whites
½ cup blackcurrant jam or jelly
3 drops orange extract
Juice and zest of ½ lemon
½ tsp vanilla extract

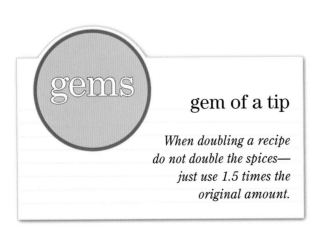

gems

gem of a tip

*When doubling a recipe
do not double the spices—
just use 1.5 times the
original amount.*

1. Preheat oven to 250°F. Line four 8- × 4-inch loaf pans with parchment paper.
2. In small bowl combine GEMS flour, baking soda, cinnamon, guar gum and cloves and set aside.
3. In very large bowl cream butter and brown sugar. Add egg whites and beat until mixture is light and fluffy.
4. Blend in jam or jelly, orange extract, lemon juice, zest and vanilla.
5. Add dry ingredients to egg mixture, beating until smooth.
6. Gradually fold fruit and nut mixture into batter, stirring until thoroughly mixed.
7. Spoon mixture into prepared pans and bake 1½ to 1¾ hours.
8. Cool completely before removing from pan. If desired, drizzle top of cake with rum or brandy.
9. Leave parchment paper on cake and wrap tightly in plastic wrap.
10. Though the cake may be eaten fresh, flavours improve if left to ripen in a cool area for a minimum of 3 weeks.

YIELD: Four 8- × 4-inch fruitcakes (total weight 6½ lb)

LIGHT FRUITCAKE

This is a delicious, light-coloured fruitcake.

FRUIT AND NUT MIXTURE

In a very large bowl combine the following
fruit and nuts:

1 cup golden raisins

½ cup apricots (chopped in ½-inch pieces)

½ cup dried pineapple (chopped in
½-inch pieces)

1 cup dates, pitted and coarsely chopped

1 cup glacé fruitcake mix

1 cup glacé coarsely chopped red cherries

1½ cups slivered almonds

BATTER

1¼ cups GEMS flour (reserve ¼ cup)

1 tsp baking powder

½ tsp guar gum

¼ tsp salt

½ cup soft butter

¼ cup granulated sugar

3 egg whites

1 tsp vanilla extract

2 Tbsp rum (or apple juice with 1 tsp rum
flavouring)

1. Preheat oven to 250°F. Line three 8- × 4-inch loaf pans with parchment paper.
2. In small bowl combine the 1 cup GEMS flour, baking powder, guar gum and
   salt and set aside.
3. In large mixing bowl cream butter and brown sugar. Add egg whites and beat
   until light and fluffy. Mix in vanilla and rum or rum-flavoured apple juice.
4. Add flour mixture to egg/butter mixture and beat until smooth.
5. Add the reserved ¼ cup GEMS flour to the fruit/nut mixture and stir to coat
   fruit. Slowly stir fruit/nut mixture into batter until thoroughly mixed. Spoon
   into prepared pans.
6. Bake approximately to 1 to 1½ hours. Cool completely before removing
   from pan. If desired, drizzle some brandy or rum overtop of cake.

7. Leaving parchment paper on cake, wrap tightly with plastic wrap and store in a cool place or refrigerator.

8. This cake can be eaten fresh but flavours improve if left to ripen in a cool area for a minimum of 2 weeks.

YIELD: Three 8- × 4-inch fruitcakes (total weight 4½ lb)

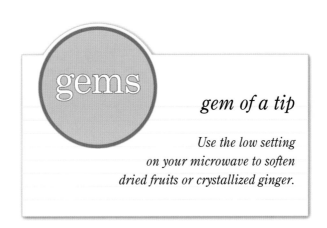

gems

gem of a tip

Use the low setting on your microwave to soften dried fruits or crystallized ginger.

MINCEMEAT FRUITCAKE

This is easy—it doesn't require ripening—
and you can't taste the mincemeat.

2½ cups mincemeat

1½ cups red glacé cherries

1 cup glacé fruitcake mix

1 cup slivered almonds

1¾ cups GEMS flour

1 tsp baking soda

1 Tbsp instant coffee powder

1 tsp ground cinnamon

½ tsp ground allspice

½ tsp guar gum

⅓ cup soft butter

¼ cup brown sugar

3 egg whites

1 Tbsp molasses

1 Tbsp brandy

1 tsp vanilla extract

1. Preheat oven to 275°F. Line bottom and sides of one 8- × 8- × 3-inch cake pan or two 8- × 4-inch loaf pans with parchment paper.
2. Combine mincemeat, cherries, diced fruitcake mix and almonds. Stir to mix.
3. In small bowl blend GEMS flour, baking soda, coffee, cinnamon, allspice and guar gum.
4. In large mixing bowl cream butter and brown sugar. Add egg whites and beat until light and fluffy. Add molasses, brandy and vanilla.
5. Add flour ingredients to egg mixture beating until blended.
6. Add fruit/nut mixture to batter and mix thoroughly.
7. Spoon into prepared pans. Bake loaves for 1¼ to 1½ hours and square cake for 1½ to 2 hours.
8. Cool completely before removing from pan.
9. Leave parchment paper on cake, wrap tightly with plastic wrap and store in refrigerator.

YIELD: One 8-× 8-inch fruitcake or two 8- × 4-inch fruitcakes (total weight 3 lb)

ORANGE DELIGHT CUPCAKES WITH BUTTER FROSTING

The citrus adds a note of freshness.

¾ cup plus 2 Tbsp GEMS flour
⅓ cup quinoa flour
1½ tsp baking powder
¼ tsp guar gum
¼ tsp salt
3 Tbsp soft butter
⅓ cup plus 1 Tbsp granulated sugar
1 egg

⅓ cup milk
½ tsp finely grated orange zest

BUTTER FROSTING
Cream 2 Tbsp soft butter with 1¼ cups icing sugar. Add 1 Tbsp orange juice and ¼ tsp grated orange zest. Blend thoroughly.

1. Preheat oven to 350°F. Line muffin tin with 12 medium baking cups.
2. In small bowl combine GEMS flour, quinoa flour, baking powder, guar gum and salt and set aside.
3. In mixing bowl, cream butter and sugar. Add egg and beat until mixture is light and fluffy.
4. Add dry ingredients alternately with the milk and beat until smooth. Stir in orange zest.
5. Spoon ¼ cup batter into each cup. Bake 15 to 18 minutes.
6. Cool completely before frosting.

YIELD: 12 medium cupcakes

GOLDEN CUPCAKES

These are tasty and moist.

1 cup brown rice flour
½ cup quinoa flour
2 tsp baking powder
½ tsp guar gum
½ tsp salt

¾ cup milk
½ cup granulated sugar
¼ cup vegetable oil
2 tsp vanilla extract
¼ tsp almond extract

1. Preheat oven to 350°F. Line muffin tin with 12 large baking cups.
2. In mixing bowl combine brown rice and quinoa flours, baking powder, guar gum and salt.
3. In 2-cup measure combine milk, sugar, vegetable oil, vanilla and almond extract.
4. Add liquid ingredients to dry ingredients and beat with mixer until smooth.
5. Spoon batter evenly between baking cups.
6. Bake 15 to 18 minutes.

YIELD: 12 large cupcakes

EGG FREE

COCONUT CUPCAKES

These rich cupcakes have good flavour and texture.

1¼ cups GEMS flour
2 tsp baking powder
¼ tsp guar gum
¼ tsp salt
1 cup coconut milk

½ cup granulated sugar
1 tsp vanilla extract
½ cup unsweetened medium or long
   shredded coconut

1. Preheat oven to 350° F. Line muffin tin with 9 large baking cups.
2. In small bowl combine GEMS flour, baking powder, guar gum and salt and set aside.
3. In medium-sized mixing bowl combine coconut milk, sugar and vanilla. Add dry ingredients and beat until smooth.
4. Add shredded coconut and stir until blended.
5. Spoon batter evenly between baking cups.
6. Bake 23 to 25 minutes. Place on rack to cool.

YIELD: 9 large cupcakes

EGG & DAIRY FREE

CHOCOLATE RASPBERRY CUPCAKES

Flavours of chocolate and raspberry combine beautifully.

¾ cup GEMS flour

½ tsp baking soda

½ tsp guar gum

¼ tsp baking powder

⅛ tsp salt

¼ cup cocoa

¼ cup hot water

¾ cup pure raspberry jam

2 Tbsp soft butter

1 egg

1. Preheat oven to 400°F. Line muffin tin with 10 large baking cups.
2. In mixing bowl blend GEMS flour, baking soda, guar gum, baking powder and salt and set aside.
3. In another bowl blend cocoa and hot water. Add raspberry jam and butter and beat until blended.
4. Combine cocoa mixture with dry ingredients and beat until smooth. Add egg and beat one minute more.
5. Spoon ¼ cup batter into each baking cup. Bake 15 to 18 minutes. Place on rack to cool.

YIELD: 10 large cupcakes

OLD-FASHIONED CAKE DOUGHNUTS

A doughnut pan is a rectangular pan with six doughnut-shaped depressions.

¾ cup GEMS flour

½ cup brown rice flour

¼ cup bean flour (preferably white)

¼ tsp guar gum

⅓ cup granulated sugar

1 Tbsp baking powder

¼ tsp ground cinnamon

¼ tsp ground nutmeg

½ tsp salt

2 Tbsp melted butter

⅔ cup milk

1 tsp vanilla extract

1. Preheat oven to 325°F. Lightly grease doughnut pan.
2. In mixing bowl combine GEMS flour, brown rice flour, bean flour, guar gum, sugar, baking powder, cinnamon, nutmeg and salt.
3. In separate bowl blend butter, milk and vanilla. Add to dry ingredients and beat until blended.
4. Fill each doughnut depression with ⅓ cup batter. Bake 15 minutes.
5. To sugar-coat: shake warm doughnuts, one at a time, in a paper bag with ¼ cup granulated sugar and ⅛ tsp cinnamon. Alternatively, sprinkle generously with icing sugar just prior to serving.

YIELD: 6 doughnuts

EGG FREE

Pictured on page 120

GLAZED CHOCOLATE CAKE DOUGHNUTS

The chocolate glaze is a nice finish.

1 cup GEMS flour
⅓ cup bean or quinoa flour
¼ cup cocoa
1 tsp baking soda
¼ tsp guar gum
¼ tsp salt
½ cup granulated sugar
1 tsp vanilla extract
¾ cup milk
1 Tbsp melted butter

GLAZE
½ square unsweetened chocolate, melted ¼ tsp vanilla extract, 1¼ cups icing sugar and approximately 2 Tbsp milk. Combine first three ingredients until thoroughly mixed. Slowly stir in milk, mixing until smooth and slightly thin. Spread while glaze is warm.

1. Preheat oven to 325°F. Lightly grease doughnut pan (see Old-Fashioned Cake Doughnuts, page 141).
2. In mixing bowl blend GEMS flour with bean or quinoa flour, cocoa, baking soda, guar gum, salt and set aside.
3. In separate bowl blend sugar, vanilla, milk and melted butter. Beat until thoroughly blended.
4. Add milk mixture to dry ingredients and beat until smooth.
5. Fill each doughnut depression with ⅓ cup batter. Bake 15 minutes.
6. While still warm, spread doughnuts with a thin layer of glaze. Place on rack to cool.
7. Repeat process with remaining batter.

YIELD: 6 doughnuts

EGG FREE

Pictured on page 120

GEM BITS

*Though these doughnuts are deep-fried not baked,
they are too good to leave out!*

⅔ cup brown rice flour

3 Tbsp tapioca starch

2 tsp baking powder

¼ tsp ground nutmeg

¼ tsp salt

⅔ cup well-mashed, baked russet potato

⅓ cup granulated sugar

2 Tbsp water

1 egg

¼ tsp vanilla extract

NOTE

A baked russet potato has a very dry texture, which allows these doughnuts to keep moist.

1. Heat approximately 2 inches of vegetable oil to 350°F in small saucepan. A toothpick dipped in the oil should sizzle when oil is at the correct temperature.
2. Blend the brown rice flour, tapioca starch, baking powder, nutmeg and salt and set aside.
3. In mixing bowl combine mashed potato, sugar, water, egg and vanilla and beat until smooth.
4. Blend dry ingredients into mashed potato mixture and beat until smooth.
5. Drop tablespoonful of dough into the hot oil and cook about 2 minutes, turning doughnut over with a fork halfway through.
6. Remove to cooling rack that is lined with paper towel. Roll in icing sugar or granulated sugar just before serving.

YIELD: 3½ dozen

DAIRY FREE

Lemon Meringue Pie, page 152

Pies & Tarts

Maple Pecan Pie, page 158

PIES AND TARTS

» Brown rice flour, with its light colour and mild flavour, is perfect for pastry.

» The advantages of using brown rice flour over wheat flour for pastry are that rice flour pastry remains tender no matter how much it is handled, requires less fat and is less subject to shrinkage.

» Guar gum will decrease the flakiness of your pastry.

» Pie or tart shells can be frozen, baked or unbaked.

» The trimmings from leftover pastry can be used to make quick and easy miniature tart shells.

» Make your own crust protectors with aluminum foil to prevent over-browning the edge.

» Double crust pies, being rich and heavy, are often served in the winter months.

» For a top crust with extra appeal, brush on egg wash then sprinkle with granulated sugar.

DOUBLE CRUST PIE

There is no trick to pastry making, just practice.

3 cups brown rice flour
1 tsp baking powder
½ tsp salt
⅔ cup cold butter or lard

1 egg
⅓ cup plus 1 Tbsp water
1 well-beaten egg
Coarse granulated sugar

1. Combine dry ingredients in bowl. With pastry blender cut in butter or lard until mixture resembles coarse meal. Blend egg with water and gradually add to flour mixture until mixture is moist enough to stick together. Form into two balls.
2. Place one ball of pastry between two sheets of waxed paper. Roll pastry from the centre outwards to size desired. Remove top sheet of waxed paper and quickly invert pastry over pie plate. Pastry gradually releases from waxed paper. Discard the waxed paper. Trim and repair pie shell where needed.
3. Add trimmings to the remaining ball and, using the above method, roll out the top crust.
4. With a pastry brush coat the interior of the pie shell with the beaten egg. This acts as a sealant between the filling and pastry and prevents a soggy crust.
5. Add the filling and lightly brush beaten egg along the outside rim of the filled bottom pie crust. This will help bind the top and bottom crusts together.
6. Invert the top crust over the filling. Press top and bottom crusts firmly around the rim of the pan. Trim pastry. Use remnants to make any repairs and to build up a thicker edge around pie.
7. Flute crust around its border with fingertips to make a decorative edge, or press with tines of a fork. Brush top crust with a thin layer of beaten egg and sprinkle with coarse granulated sugar. With a sharp knife cut three evenly spaced slits in top crust for steam to escape. Bake as directed in recipe.

YIELD: Double crust for 8- or 9-inch pie

SINGLE CRUST PIE

Pastry uses simple ingredients.

Prepare half the pastry for a Double Crust Pie (steps 1 to 3), page 147.

1. Use the pastry trimmings to make a thicker edge. Crimp border with fingertips or press with fork tines.
2. UNBAKED   Add fillings such as pumpkin and rhubarb custard and bake according to recipe directions.
3. PREBAKED PIE SHELL   To prevent air bubbles from forming beneath the pastry during baking, fit a same size pie plate, or next size smaller, over unbaked crust. If you have used an aluminum foil pie plate, set another foil pie plate overtop and fill the bottom with dried peas, beans or rice to keep it in place.
4. Bake at 450°F for 10 to 12 minutes. Cool and fill with any precooked filling such as lemon, chocolate, strawberry, etc.

YIELD: Single crust for 8- or 9-inch pie

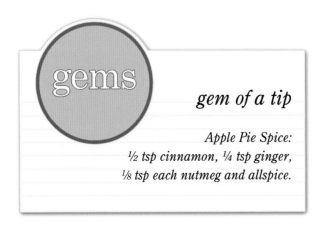

gems

gem of a tip

Apple Pie Spice:
½ tsp cinnamon, ¼ tsp ginger,
⅛ tsp each nutmeg and allspice.

TART SHELLS

Use pastry trimmings for quick mini tarts.

Prepare pastry for Double Crust Pie, page 147, Step 1, but form into one ball instead of two.

1. Preheat oven to 450°F.
2. Place pastry ball between two sheets of waxed paper. Roll to ⅛-inch thickness.
3. Cut 3-inch rounds of pastry and line 2½-inch diameter shallow tart pans, or cut 2-inch rounds for mini muffin tins. Prick bottom and sides of pastry with a fork.
4. PREBAKED   Bake the empty tart shells at 450°F for 8 minutes. Place on rack to cool.

    UNBAKED   Add filling to unbaked tart shells and bake according to directions.

    FROZEN   Purchase aluminum foil tart pans. Fit a 3-inch round of pastry in foil pan, prick with fork, stack one on top of the other, wrap firmly in a freezer-proof bag and freeze. Place frozen tart shells on baking sheet and bake for 10 minutes at 450°F, or add filling and bake according to recipe directions.

    YIELD: 8 to 12 tart shells depending on size of pan

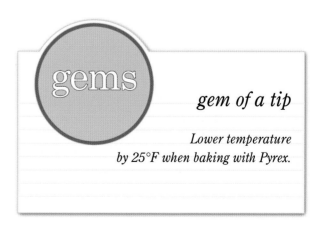

gems

gem of a tip

Lower temperature by 25°F when baking with Pyrex.

FRESH FRUIT PIE

Use this recipe for all fresh fruit or berry pies.

Prepare prebaked 8-inch pie shell from Single Crust Pie, page 148.

5 cups whole fresh fruit	1 cup water
⅔ cup granulated sugar	1 Tbsp lemon juice
¼ cup cornstarch	2 Tbsp butter

1. Coarsely chop 2½ cups fresh fruit. Small berries may be left whole.
2. In saucepan mix sugar and cornstarch. Add water and mix until blended. Add chopped fruit and cook over medium heat until mixture is thick and clear. Remove from heat and add lemon juice and butter.
3. Stir in remaining fruit. Add a little more sugar if the filling is not sweet enough.
4. Pour into prebaked pie shell and chill.

YIELD: One 8-inch pie (6 servings)

AUTUMN APPLE PIE

The taste of lightly spiced tart apples encased in a golden pastry.

Prepare pastry for Double Crust Pie, page 147.

2 lb or 6 cups firm/tart apples (peeled,
    cored and cut into ¼-inch slices)
1 Tbsp lemon juice
½ cup granulated sugar

½ tsp ground cinnamon
¼ tsp ground ginger
⅛ tsp ground nutmeg
⅛ tsp ground allspice

1. Preheat oven to 400°F. Line an 8-inch pie plate with half the rolled pastry.
2. In large bowl sprinkle lemon juice over apples. Combine spices and sugar
    and add to apples, mixing to evenly coat.
3. Slide apple mixture into pie shell. Finish pie according to directions for
    making a Double Crust Pie.
4. Place in lower third of oven and bake 20 minutes. Reduce heat to 350°F
    and bake a further 30 to 35 minutes.
5. Place on rack to cool.

YIELD: One 8-inch pie (6 servings)

LEMON MERINGUE PIE

A wonderful tangy lemon filling.

Prepare prebaked 9-inch pie shell from Single Crust Pie, page 148.

FILLING

1⅓ cups water

⅞ cup granulated sugar

6 Tbsp cornstarch

3 large egg yolks, lightly beaten

3 Tbsp butter

Juice and grated zest of 2 large lemons

1. Combine water, sugar and cornstarch in saucepan and cook until thick.
2. To prevent eggs curdling remove ½ cup of the hot mixture and blend with the egg yolks.
3. Pour egg yolk mixture into thickened cornstarch mixture and stir until blended. Simmer for 5 minutes. Remove from heat and stir in butter and juice and zest of lemons.
4. Pour hot filling into pie shell and immediately top with meringue, facing page.

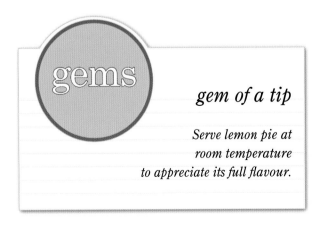

gems

gem of a tip

Serve lemon pie at room temperature to appreciate its full flavour.

MERINGUE

3 egg whites

¼ tsp cream of tartar

6 Tbsp granulated sugar

1. Preheat oven to 375°F.
2. Beat egg whites until foamy. Add cream of tartar and beat until soft peaks form.
3. Continue to beat and add 1 Tbsp sugar at a time until egg whites are very stiff and sugar has dissolved (no sugar granules should be felt between thumb and index finger).
4. Spoon meringue over warm pie filling. Spread meringue to edge of crust to form a seal and prevent shrinkage during baking.
5. Bake 15 minutes.
6. Place on rack to cool.

YIELD: One 9-inch pie (8 servings)

Pictured on page 144

CLASSIC RAISIN PIE

Pioneers used raisins to replace fruits not in season.

Prepare pastry for a Double Crust Pie, page 147.

2½ cups seedless sultana raisins, rinsed

1½ cups water

½ cup packed brown sugar

3 Tbsp cornstarch

2 Tbsp vinegar

⅓ cup orange juice

1 cup evaporated milk or cream

1. Preheat oven to 375°F. Line 8-inch pie plate with half the rolled pastry.
2. Place raisins in saucepan with water and brown sugar. Simmer 10 minutes.
3. Mix cornstarch with vinegar and orange juice and slowly add to raisin mixture, cooking until thick. Stir in evaporated milk or cream.
4. Spoon raisin mixture into pie shell. Finish pie according to directions for making a Double Crust Pie.
5. Place in lower third of oven and bake for 35 minutes.
6. Place on rack to cool.

YIELD: One 8-inch pie (8 servings)

MINCEMEAT PIE AND TARTS

Stays fresh and keeps longer than most pies.

1. Follow recipe for Classic Raisin Pie, facing page, replacing filling with 3 cups prepared mincemeat.
2. Bake according to recipe.

YIELD: One 8-inch pie (8 servings)

TARTS

Three cups mincemeat will yield 10 to 18 tarts depending on size of pan.

1. Refer to recipe on page 149 to make tart shells. Doubling the amount of pastry (i.e., using the recipe for Double Crust Pie, page 147) will be necessary for this number of tarts. You will end up with leftover pastry—well wrapped, it freezes successfully.
2. Spoon 2½ Tbsp mincemeat into each unbaked tart shell.
3. Bake at 350°F for 15 minutes for regular tarts, and 10 minutes for mini tarts.

YIELD: 10 to 18 tarts depending on size of pan

PUMPKIN PIE AND TARTS

Lightly grease pie plate and make a pastry-free pumpkin custard.

Prepare pastry for Single Crust Pie, page 148.

2 cups canned pumpkin

1 cup evaporated whole milk

2 eggs

½ cup granulated sugar

½ tsp salt

¼ tsp ground ginger

¼ tsp ground nutmeg

⅛ tsp ground cloves

1. Preheat oven to 325°F. Line 9-inch pie plate with rolled pastry.
2. In a large bowl combine pumpkin, milk, eggs, sugar, salt and spices and beat with hand mixer until smooth.
3. Pour into pie shell. Bake 1 hour.
4. Place on rack to cool.

YIELD: One 9-inch pie (6 servings)

TARTS

Half the filling for the above pumpkin pie will yield 15 tarts.

1. Refer to recipe on page 149 to make tart shells. Doubling the amount of pastry (i.e., using the recipe for Double Crust Pie, page 147) will be necessary for this number of tarts. You may end up with leftover pastry—well wrapped, it freezes successfully.
2. Prepare half the filling for Pumpkin Pie.
3. Spoon 3 Tbsp filling into unbaked tart shells.
4. Bake at 375°F for 18 to 20 minutes.

YIELD: 15 tarts

RHUBARB CUSTARD PIE

A rich, creamy custard pie filled with fresh rhubarb.

Prepare pastry for Single Crust Pie, page 148.

4 cups chopped fresh rhubarb (about
 ½-inch pieces)
⅔ cup granulated sugar
3 Tbsp brown rice flour

1 beaten egg
¾ cup cream
1 tsp grated orange zest
Pinch salt

1. Preheat oven to 425°F. Line 9-inch pie plate with rolled pastry.
2. Place rhubarb in bowl, toss with mixture of sugar and brown rice flour and spoon into pie shell.
3. In small bowl mix egg, cream, zest and salt and pour over rhubarb.
4. Bake 15 minutes then reduce heat to 350°F and continue baking until knife inserted comes out clean, about 15 minutes.
5. Place on rack to cool.

YIELD: One 9-inch pie (8 servings)

MAPLE PECAN PIE

Decadent and delicious!

Prepare a prebaked 9-inch pie shell from Single Crust Pie, page 148.

2½ cups toasted pecans, coarsely chopped

¾ cup maple syrup

⅓ cup pure brown rice syrup (a thick, not-too-sweet syrup available at natural food stores)

1 Tbsp vanilla extract

½ Tbsp minced fresh ginger

¼ tsp salt

¼ cup ground flax

1½ tsp tapioca starch

⅓ cup soy milk

A few pecan halves to decorate top (optional)

1. Spread pecans on baking sheet and toast at 325°F for 12 minutes. Cool.
2. Increase oven temperature to 350°F. Transfer toasted pecans to mixing bowl.
3. In medium saucepan, combine maple syrup, rice syrup, vanilla, fresh ginger and salt. Simmer mixture for 5 minutes then remove from heat. Cool to room temperature.
4. Combine ground flax, tapioca starch and soy milk with the maple syrup mixture and pour into blender. Blend until smooth.
5. Pour blended liquid over the pecans, mix well and pour into prebaked pie shell. Decorate top with pecan halves if desired.
6. Bake 30 minutes or until the filling has firmed.
7. Place on rack to cool.

YIELD: One 9-inch pie (10 servings)

EGG & DAIRY FREE

Pictured on page 146

PEAR FLAN WITH WALNUT CRUST

Make this scrumptious flan when pears are in season.

CRUST

2 cups walnuts

½ cup GEMS flour

3 Tbsp packed brown sugar

¼ tsp salt

¼ tsp ground cinnamon

About 3 Tbsp water (as needed)

FILLING

6 average-sized firm, ripe Anjou
   or Bartlett pears

3 Tbsp packed brown sugar

2 Tbsp brown rice flour

¾ tsp ground cinnamon

Grated zest of lemon

1 Tbsp fresh lemon juice

Pinch salt

1. Generously grease 9- or 10-inch pie plate.
2. Place walnuts and ¼ cup of the GEMS flour in a food processor with steel blade attachment. Pulse on and off until the nuts are ground to a fine meal. If using a blender grind the nuts in three or four batches rather than all at once.
3. Transfer walnuts to a bowl. Add the other ¼ cup GEMS flour, brown sugar, salt and cinnamon and mix until evenly distributed. Add water 1 Tbsp at a time, mixing after each addition, until the dough holds together when squeezed (it should not be sticky).

continues

4.   Press the dough evenly into the bottom and sides of prepared pie plate and set aside while preparing filling.

5.   Preheat oven to 375°F.

6.   Peel, core and slice pears and place in mixing bowl.

7.   Combine the brown sugar, brown rice flour, cinnamon, salt and lemon zest and sprinkle over the pears, tossing slices gently to coat.

8.   Spread filling (if desired arrange pear slices in a concentric pattern) into the unbaked crust and drizzle with the lemon juice.

9.   Bake 35 minutes. It may be necessary to protect edges of crust with aluminum foil to prevent over-browning.

YIELD: One 9- or 10-inch flan (10 servings)

EGG, DAIRY & FAT FREE

CREAM CHEESE PASTRY

This is a tender, delicious pastry.

1½ cups brown rice flour
½ tsp salt

⅓ cup regular cream cheese (light cream
    cheese makes pastry tough)
2 Tbsp butter

1. Preheat oven to 375°F.
2. Combine ingredients in food processor and pulse until mixed. Form into
   a ball and lightly knead by hand. Divide into two balls.
3. Pinch off tablespoon-sized pieces of dough and press into mini muffin tin.
4. Bake tart shells for 10 minutes. Place on rack to cool.

YIELD: 24 mini tart shells

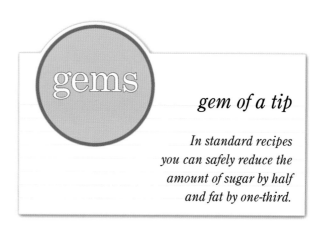

gems

gem of a tip

*In standard recipes
you can safely reduce the
amount of sugar by half
and fat by one-third.*

PETITE BUTTER TARTS

Tasty little nuggets that pack a wallop!

Prepare pastry (but do not bake) for 24 mini Tart Shells, page 149, or Cream Cheese Pastry, page 161.

1 egg	3 Tbsp melted butter
⅓ cup granulated sugar	2 Tbsp milk
½ cup sultana raisins	¼ cup chopped walnuts
½ tsp vanilla extract	

1. Preheat oven to 375°F.
2. In small saucepan beat egg. Add sugar, raisins, vanilla, butter and milk. Bring to a boil and cook 1 minute. Stir in nuts.
3. Drop 1½ tsp filling into each tart shell.
4. Bake for 10 to 12 minutes.
5. Place on rack to cool.

YIELD: 24 mini tarts

QUICK AND EASY LEMON TARTS

These are pure bliss!

Prepare pastry for 12 prebaked 2½-inch diameter Tart Shells, page 149.

14 oz can sweetened condensed milk	1½ tsp grated lemon zest
¼ cup fresh lemon juice	½ cup firm plain yogurt

1. In mixing bowl combine condensed milk, lemon juice and zest. Fold in yogurt and chill thoroughly. This mixture can be stored in the fridge up to a week.
2. Spoon into prepared tart shells. Serve immediately.

YIELD: 12 tarts

TRADITIONAL LEMON TARTS

Enjoy the lemony goodness with each bite.

Prepare 12 prebaked 2½-inch diameter Tart Shells, page 149.
Prepare half the filling recipe for Lemon Meringue Pie, page 152.

1. Spoon 2 Tbsp of hot filling into each tart shell. Cool.
2. Lightly sprinkle with icing sugar just before serving.

YIELD: 12 tarts

RASPBERRY GLAZED TARTS

Appealing to look at and mouth-wateringly good.

Prepare 12 prebaked 2½-inch diameter Tart Shells, page 149.

15 oz pkg frozen sweetened raspberries	1 Tbsp granulated sugar
2½ Tbsp cornstarch	

1. Thaw fruit, reserving juice.
2. Add water to the juice to make 1 cup of liquid.
3. In a saucepan mix cornstarch and sugar, add juice and cook over medium heat for 5 minutes. Remove from heat and cool slightly. Fold in drained fruit.
4. Spoon into prebaked tart shells and chill.
5. Serve with a dollop of whipped cream.

YIELD: 12 tarts

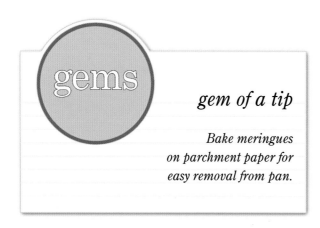

gems

gem of a tip

Bake meringues on parchment paper for easy removal from pan.

DELUXE FRUIT TARTS

This is a wonderfully delicious tart.

Prepare 12 prebaked 2½-inch diameter Tart Shells, page 149.

3 oz pkg vanilla pudding mix (not instant)
2 cups milk
6 oz pkg cream cheese
2 Tbsp granulated sugar

FRESH FRUIT TOPPING
Fresh fruit, sliced, coarsely chopped (leave
   berries whole)
Granulated sugar

NOTE
For Fresh Fruit Topping, use a single fruit or
   a medley of berries, sliced strawberries,
   kiwi and peaches.

1. Combine pudding mix and milk and cook according to package directions.
   Remove from heat.
2. Cut cream cheese into small pieces and add to hot pudding. Stir until
   cheese is melted.
3. Spoon into tart shells. Chill.
4. Arrange lightly sugared fruit on top of each tart and serve immediately.

YIELD: 12 tarts

Chocolate Raspberry Mousse, page 175

Desserts

Cream Puffs, facing page

DESERTS

» When you are hosting a special dinner party, allow an hour or more before serving dessert. Your guests will be able to really enjoy a rich dessert when there has been a break between dinner and the final course.

» Crumbles, crisps and streusels contain three basic ingredients: flour, butter and sugar.

» Crisps have oatmeal added to the basic ingredients while streusels have nuts added.

» When fresh fruits are not available, rehydrated dried, frozen or canned fruits are excellent alternatives.

» A torte is a European cake divided into several layers. Sponge cake or meringue is usually used for the layers. A thick custard or whipped cream is used for the filling.

» The lightest and easiest-to-prepare desserts are fruits, whether served fresh, stewed or baked.

CREAM PUFFS

Cream puffs are delightful treats and easy to make.

½ cup brown rice flour
1½ Tbsp cornstarch
⅛ tsp guar gum
½ cup water

¼ cup soft butter
2 eggs
Slightly sweetened, vanilla-flavoured
   whipped cream for filling

1. Preheat oven to 425°F. Line baking sheet with parchment paper.
2. In small bowl combine brown rice flour, cornstarch and guar gum.
3. In saucepan bring the water and butter to a boil. Remove from heat. Add flour quickly while beating with hand mixer.
4. Return pan to heat and continue to beat until mixture forms a ball. Remove from heat. Cool 5 minutes.
5. In same pot add eggs, one at a time, and beat until mixture is fluffy.
6. Drop dollops of dough (3 Tbsp each) on baking sheet 3 inches apart.
7. Bake for 15 minutes then reduce heat to 375°F and bake for 10 more minutes.
8. Turn off heat, open oven door slightly and leave cream puffs in the oven for 30 more minutes to dry out further. Cool on racks.
9. To serve, cut cream puffs in half and fill with whipped cream.

YIELD: 8 cream puffs

Pictured opposite

ÉCLAIRS

These are impressive.

Make same dough as for Cream Puffs, previous page.

CREAM FILLING
1 cup milk
3 Tbsp granulated sugar
2 Tbsp cornstarch
1 egg yolk
1 Tbsp butter
½ tsp vanilla extract
⅓ cup whipping cream, whipped

1. In small saucepan combine ¾ cup milk and sugar. Bring to a boil over medium heat. While heating whisk cornstarch, egg yolk and remaining milk. Mix ¼ cup of the hot milk into egg yolk mixture stirring to blend then pour back into hot milk. Bring to a boil and boil 30 seconds.
2. Remove from heat and add butter and vanilla. Cool completely before folding in whipped cream.

FILLING OPTION
For a quick cream filling use instant vanilla pudding mix (or flavour of choice). Replace the milk with light or heavy cream, depending on how rich you want it to be.

THIN CHOCOLATE GLAZE
Melt 1 square unsweetened chocolate and 1 tsp butter over hot water. Remove fromheat and blend in 1 cup icing sugar and 2 Tbsp boiling water, beating only until smooth.

1. Take ¼ cup of dough and shape into a 4-inch length on parchment-lined baking sheet. Space éclairs approximately 2 inches apart.
2. Bake as directed for Cream Puffs. When cool, slice in half and fill with Cream Filling. Frost with Thin Chocolate Glaze.

YIELD: 6 éclairs

DELUXE BLACK FOREST TORTE

Make this spectacular dessert for a very special occasion.

CAKE

¾ cup fine dry gluten-free bread crumbs	8 egg yolks (room temperature)
½ cup almond meal	1 Tbsp water
½ cup GEMS flour	1 cup granulated sugar
⅓ cup cocoa	½ tsp almond extract
1 whole egg	8 egg whites (room temperature)

1. Preheat oven to 350°F. Lightly grease two 9-inch round cake pans and line with parchment paper.
2. In a small bowl blend the bread crumbs, almond meal, GEMS flour and cocoa and set aside.
3. In large bowl combine whole egg, egg yolks and water. Adding sugar gradually, beat the eggs on high until mixture gets very thick, about 5 or 6 minutes.
4. Fold dry ingredients into the eggs using a wire whisk.
5. In large bowl beat egg whites with almond extract until stiff but not dry. Quickly, but gently, fold egg whites into first mixture. Divide batter evenly between pans.
6. Bake 20 to 25 minutes or until cake is springy when touched.
7. Cool a few minutes then turn out on racks to finish cooling.
8. Before slicing each cake horizontally into two equal layers, insert toothpicks in six places around circumference to guide the knife as you cut. Keep cakes covered until ready to use.

continues

gems

gem of a tip

To make bread crumbs, slice stale bread, dry in a slow oven, crush with rolling pin, store in cupboard.

FILLING

2 cups frozen pitted sour red cherries,
   not thawed

2 Tbsp water

¼ cup granulated sugar

1 Tbsp cornstarch

Pinch salt

⅛ tsp almond extract

OPTION

Substitute canned cherry pie filling for the
   first five ingredients. Add almond extract.
   The canned cherry pie filling is already
   thickened so there is no need to cook it.

1. In small saucepan combine cherries and water. Cook over low heat for 10 minutes or until cherry juices begin to form. Can also be microwaved on medium power for 4 minutes.
2. In small bowl mix the sugar, cornstarch and salt. Add to cherries and cook until the juice is thick. Remove from heat and stir in almond extract. Cool.

12-HOUR WHIPPED CREAM TOPPING

1 envelope (1 Tbsp) unflavoured gelatin

2 Tbsp cold water

2½ cups whipping cream

⅓ cup icing sugar

Pinch salt

1 tsp vanilla extract

¼ tsp almond extract

1. In a small dish soften the gelatin in the water.
2. Set dish in a pan of simmering water and heat until gelatin dissolves. Remove from heat and keep warm.
3. In a large mixing bowl beat the whipping cream, icing sugar, salt and extracts until just beginning to thicken.
4. Reduce speed and, in a very thin stream, slowly add gelatin, beating until stiff peaks form.
5. Cover and store in refrigerator until ready to use.

ASSEMBLING THE CAKE

1. If desired, sprinkle each layer of cake with a little kirsch.
2. Place bottom layer of cake on serving platter and cover with the cherry filling to within ½ inch of the margin.
3. Spread one-quarter of the whipped cream over cherries.
4. Cover with the second layer of cake and spread with another one-quarter of the cream.
5. Repeat Step 4 with third layer of cake.
6. Place final cake layer on top and ice with remaining whipped cream.
7. Pile some chocolate curls in centre of cake and decorate border with stemmed maraschino cherries.
8. Chill cake before serving.

CHOCOLATE CURLS

1. Add 1½ cups chocolate chips to ¼ cup soft butter. Melt in microwave and stir until smooth. Pour mixture into a small greased plastic container and refrigerate for 1 hour.
2. When solid remove chocolate block from container. Use a vegetable peeler to make perfect chocolate curls.
3. Refrigerate until firm. Use a wooden skewer to delicately pile chocolate curls on centre of cake.

YIELD: One 9-inch double-layer cake (12 servings)

APPLE CRUMBLE

*For a touch of colour sprinkle ¾ cup
dried cranberries over apples.*

5 large apples (peeled, cored and sliced)
1 Tbsp lemon juice
½ cup granulated sugar (divided)
½ tsp ground cinnamon

¼ tsp ground allspice
¾ cup brown rice flour
¼ cup soft butter

1. Preheat oven to 350°F. Lightly grease 8- × 8-inch pan.
2. Place apples in a large mixing bowl and sprinkle with lemon juice. Blend ¼ cup of the sugar with cinnamon and allspice, tossing to coat. Arrange apples in prepared pan.
3. In small bowl combine the remaining sugar with the brown rice flour and butter and work with fingertips until mixture resembles fine crumbs. Sprinkle evenly over apples.
4. Bake 30 to 35 minutes. Serve warm or cold with ice cream.

APPLE STREUSEL
Add ½ cup sliced almonds to the butter/sugar/flour mixture.

APPLE CRISP
Add ¾ cup gluten-free quick oats to the butter/sugar/flour mixture.

YIELD: One 8-× 8-inch pan (6 servings)

EGG FREE

CHOCOLATE RASPBERRY MOUSSE

*You know this has to be good when your son
and his friends ask for seconds.*

CASHEW CRUST

⅓ cup raw cashews

3 Tbsp granulated sugar

3 Tbsp vegetable oil

½ tsp vanilla extract

1 cup less 2 Tbsp brown rice flour

¼ tsp guar gum

⅛ tsp salt

MOUSSE

2 cups non-dairy chocolate chips

24 ounces low-fat silken tofu

⅔ cup granulated sugar

½ tsp salt

1 tsp vanilla extract

1. Preheat oven to 350°F. Lightly grease 8-inch springform pan.
2. In food processor grind cashews to form a meal. Add sugar, oil, vanilla, brown rice flour, guar gum and salt process to mix, then work with hands to complete mixing. Press mixture into prepared bottom of pan and bake 20 minutes.
3. Melt chocolate chips over simmering water. While chocolate is melting, place tofu, sugar, salt and vanilla in food processor and process until smooth.
4. Continue to process, slowly adding the melted chocolate. Blend for 2 minutes.
5. Pour mousse over baked crust and bake 50 to 55 minutes.
6. Cool 10 minutes then run knife around inside of pan. Chill.
7. To serve cut into 12 wedges. Drizzle raspberry sauce over each wedge.

continues

gems

gem of a tip

Homemade Vanilla Extract—Combine 1 vanilla bean slit lengthwise and cut into 3 pieces in 1 cup vodka for minimum 8 weeks.

THIN RASPBERRY SAUCE

2 pkg (10 oz each) frozen unsweetened raspberries

¼ cup granulated sugar

1. Thaw raspberries. Drain, reserving juice. Press berries through a sieve to remove seeds, if desired.
2. Combine raspberry pulp with sugar and reserved juice. The sauce is meant to be thin. The tang of the raspberries complements the richness of the dessert.

YIELD: One 8-inch mousse cake (12 servings)

EGG & DAIRY FREE

Pictured on page 166

CHOCOLATE FUDGE PUDDING

A simple and flavourful dessert.

1 cup GEMS flour

1 Tbsp baking powder

½ tsp salt

½ cup granulated sugar

2 Tbsp cocoa

½ cup milk

2 Tbsp vegetable oil

½ tsp vanilla extract

⅔ cup brown sugar

⅓ cup cocoa

2 cups hot water

1. Preheat oven to 350°F. Lightly grease 9- × 9-inch pan.
2. In mixing bowl blend the GEMS flour, baking powder, salt, sugar and the 2 Tbsp cocoa. Stir in milk, oil and vanilla.
3. Spread into prepared pan. Sprinkle with mixture of brown sugar and the ⅓ cup cocoa.
4. Carefully pour 2 cups hot water over entire batter and bake for 40 to 45 minutes. During baking, cake mixture rises to top and chocolate sauce settles to bottom.
5. Serve warm with vanilla ice cream.

YIELD: 6 servings

EGG FREE

LEMON CAKE PUDDING

A delicate cake in a refreshing lemon sauce.

¼ cup brown rice flour

½ cup granulated sugar

⅛ tsp salt

¼ cup lemon juice

1 Tbsp lemon zest

2 egg yolks

1½ cups milk

2 egg whites, stiffly beaten

1. Preheat oven to 350°F. Lightly grease 6-cup casserole or four custard cups.
2. In mixing bowl blend brown rice flour, sugar and salt. Add lemon juice, lemon zest, egg yolks and milk. Beat until blended.
3. Fold egg whites into cake batter.
4. Pour into prepared pan or spoon into custard cups. Set in a larger pan containing 1 inch hot water. The hot water bath will prevent the eggs from curdling.
5. Bake 40 to 45 minutes.

YIELD: 4 servings

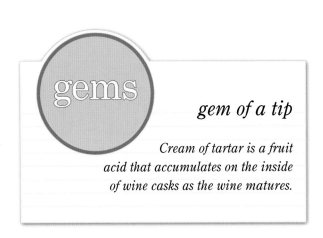

gems

gem of a tip

Cream of tartar is a fruit acid that accumulates on the inside of wine casks as the wine matures.

ALMOND CAKE

My sister Gillian brought back this delicious recipe from Norway.

2 cups almond meal
⅔ cup granulated sugar
3 egg whites
1 whole egg
¼ tsp almond extract
2 Tbsp water
2 Tbsp potato starch
2 tsp baking powder
¼ tsp salt

MOCHA-FLAVOURED TOPPING

Combine in mixing bowl: 1½ cups whipping cream, 1½ tsp cocoa, 1 tsp instant coffee dissolved in 1 tsp vanilla extract. Beat until soft peaks form.

1. Preheat oven to 325°F. Lightly grease 9-inch springform pan.
2. In mixing bowl combine the almond meal, sugar, egg whites, whole egg, almond extract and water. Beat until mixture is light and fluffy.
3. Blend in the potato starch, baking powder and salt.
4. Pour into prepared pan and bake for 20 to 25 minutes. Cool.
5. Served chilled with Mocha-Flavoured Topping.

YIELD: One 9-inch round cake (12 servings)

BOILING WATER GINGERBREAD

This mildly flavoured gingerbread is first in its class!

1¼ cups GEMS flour
1½ tsp baking powder
¾ tsp ground ginger
¾ tsp ground cinnamon
½ tsp ground nutmeg
⅛ tsp ground cloves
½ tsp guar gum
¼ tsp salt
½ cup brown sugar

⅓ cup vegetable oil
¼ cup molasses
1 egg
½ tsp baking soda
½ cup boiling water

OPTION
Add 2 Tbsp finely chopped crystallized
   ginger to cake batter.

1. Preheat oven to 350°F. Lightly grease 8- × 8-inch pan.
2. In small bowl combine GEMS flour, baking powder, ginger, cinnamon, nutmeg, cloves, guar gum and salt and set aside.
3. In mixing bowl combine brown sugar, oil, molasses, egg and beat until mixed. Add dry ingredients to molasses mixture and blend.
4. Add baking soda to the boiling water and quickly blend into flour mixture.
5. Pour into prepared pan and bake 30 minutes.
6. Serve warm with Lemon Sauce (facing page), chunky applesauce or whipped cream.

LEMON SAUCE

⅓ cup granulated sugar

1 Tbsp cornstarch

1 cup water

1 Tbsp butter

1½ Tbsp fresh lemon juice

½ tsp lemon zest

1. In small saucepan combine sugar, cornstarch and water. Cook over medium heat, stirring constantly until thickened.
2. Remove from heat and stir in butter, lemon juice and lemon zest.

YIELD: One 8- × 8-inch pan (9 servings)

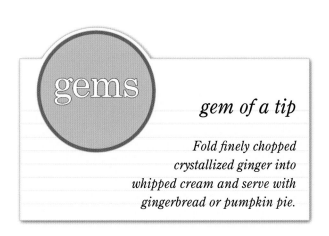

gems

gem of a tip

*Fold finely chopped
crystallized ginger into
whipped cream and serve with
gingerbread or pumpkin pie.*

PINEAPPLE UPSIDE-DOWN CAKE

Bring this eye-appealing dessert to the table.

2 Tbsp packed brown sugar
8 slices of canned pineapple, drained
4 maraschino cherries, halved
14 pecan halves
⅔ cup brown rice flour
¼ cup bean flour
3 Tbsp cornstarch
4 tsp baking powder
½ tsp salt
½ tsp guar gum
⅓ cup soft butter

½ cup granulated sugar
1 egg
⅔ cup milk
1 tsp almond extract

CHECKERBOARD VARIATION:
Replace the pineapple, cherries and pecans
with fresh or canned apricot and plum
halves, and the almond extract with
vanilla extract.

1. Preheat oven to 325° F. Lightly grease 9-inch round pan or ovenproof skillet.
2. Sprinkle bottom of pan with brown sugar. Arrange pineapple slices on top of brown sugar. Place a cherry half, cut side down, in centre of each ring. Fill in open spaces with pecans.
3. In small bowl combine the brown rice flour, bean flour, cornstarch, baking powder, salt and guar gum.
4. In medium-sized mixing bowl cream the butter and sugar. Add egg and beat with hand mixer until light and fluffy.

5. Stir in one-third of the flour mixture and then add one-half of the milk. Repeat, alternating dry and liquid ingredients, ending with the flour.
6. Stir in almond extract and pour batter over pineapple rings.
7. Bake 30 to 35 minutes.
8. Immediately turn upside-down on serving platter, leaving pan atop cake for a few minutes.

YIELD: One 9-inch round cake (9 servings)

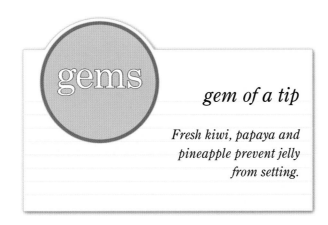

gems

gem of a tip

Fresh kiwi, papaya and pineapple prevent jelly from setting.

PAVLOVA

An elegant dessert named after the Russian ballerina Anna Pavlova.

MERINGUE
4 egg whites, room temperature
½ tsp cream of tartar
Pinch salt
¾ cup icing sugar
1 Tbsp cornstarch
1 Tbsp lemon juice

FILLING
1 cup chilled whipping cream
2 Tbsp icing sugar
⅛ tsp vanilla extract

TOPPING
Sliced strawberries and kiwi

1. Preheat oven to 200°F. With marker draw a 9-inch circle on parchment paper, turn the paper over and place on pan.
2. In large mixing bowl beat egg whites to a foam. Add cream of tartar and salt and beat until soft peaks form. Slowly beat in ½ cup of the icing sugar, 1 Tbsp at a time.
3. Mix remaining sugar with the cornstarch. Add to egg whites and beat until stiff peaks form. Fold in lemon juice.
4. Spread meringue on top of prepared circle, keeping edges of meringue a little higher than the centre.
5. Lower heat to 180°F and bake for 1½ to 2 hours. When baked, the outside of the meringue will have cracks and feel firm to touch.
6. Turn the oven off and let the meringue remain in oven a few hours or overnight to become crisp and dry.
7. Just prior to serving, pour whipping cream into bowl, add icing sugar and vanilla and beat until soft peaks form. Spread over meringue and decorate with sliced fruit. Serve immediately.

YIELD: 8 servings

CHEESECAKE

A rich-tasting, lighter version of the New York–style cheesecake.

CRUST

2 cups gluten-free cornflake crumbs

2 Tbsp granulated sugar

⅓ cup melted butter

FILLING

1½ lb creamed cottage cheese
  (about 3 cups)

½ cup granulated sugar

4 eggs

1 tsp lemon juice

TOPPING

1 cup sour cream (not light)

¼ cup granulated sugar

½ tsp vanilla extract

1. Preheat oven to 325°F. Lightly grease 9-inch springform pan.
2. In small mixing bowl blend cornflake crumbs, sugar and butter together. Press into bottom of prepared pan and refrigerate.
3. Blend cottage cheese, sugar, eggs and lemon juice until smooth. Pour into chilled crust.
4. Bake for one hour. Remove from oven and cool 20 minutes.
5. Whisk together sour cream, sugar and vanilla and spread over cake. Return to oven and bake 15 more minutes. Chill before slicing.
6. Serve topped with fresh berries.

YIELD: One 9-inch cheesecake (12 servings)

APPLE BROWN BETTY

An old-fashioned dessert using bread crumbs.

6 medium apples (peeled, cored and sliced)

2 Tbsp lemon juice

1½ cups dry gluten-free bread crumbs

¼ cup melted butter

½ cup brown sugar

1 tsp ground cinnamon

¼ tsp ground nutmeg

1. Preheat oven to 350°F. Lightly grease 6-cup casserole.
2. In mixing bowl toss apples with lemon juice.
3. In small bowl mix bread crumbs with melted butter.
4. Combine brown sugar, cinnamon and nutmeg in a small cup.
5. In bottom of casserole alternate layers of one-third bread crumb mixture, half of the sliced apples and half of the sugar/spice mix. Repeat layers. Sprinkle remaining one-third bread crumbs overtop.
6. Cover casserole and bake 30 minutes. Remove cover and bake 15 more minutes.
7. Serve warm with ice cream.

YIELD: 6 servings

EGG FREE

STRAWBERRY RHUBARB COBBLER

Cobblers are best prepared with fruits that produce lots of juice.

3 cups sliced fresh rhubarb, ½-inch pieces

3 cups hulled, sliced fresh strawberries

½ cup granulated sugar

1 Tbsp cornstarch

1⅓ cups brown rice flour

5 Tbsp granulated sugar (reserve 1 Tbsp)

½ tsp guar gum

1 Tbsp baking powder

¼ tsp salt

3 Tbsp soft butter

¾ cup milk

1. Preheat oven to 350°F. Lightly grease a 9- × 9-inch pan.
2. Place rhubarb and strawberries in a large mixing bowl. Blend the ½ cup sugar and cornstarch and sprinkle over fruit tossing to coat. Spread into bottom of prepared pan.
3. In mixing bowl blend the brown rice flour, the 4 Tbsp sugar and the guar gum, baking powder and salt.
4. Work the soft butter into the flour mixture with fingers or pastry blender until mixture resembles coarse meal.
5. Pour milk into flour mixture and stir enough to moisten. Drop heaping table-spoonsful of batter, evenly spaced, over rhubarb and strawberries.
6. Sprinkle reserved sugar overtop and bake 35 minutes or until mixture is bubbling up around edge.
7. Serve warm or cold.

YIELD: 8 servings

EGG FREE

STICKY TOFFEE PUDDING

Nothing describes this better than "yummy."

1 cup pitted and chopped dates

1 cup warm water

⅓ cup firmly packed brown sugar

2 Tbsp soft butter

¼ tsp vanilla extract

1 egg

½ cup GEMS flour

¾ tsp baking soda

1. Combine dates and water in saucepan and stir over medium heat until the dates soften. Cool.
2. Preheat oven to 350°F. Lightly grease 6 muffin cups.
3. In mixing bowl combine brown sugar and butter and beat until creamy. Add vanilla and egg and beat until light and fluffy.
4. Add softened dates and water and beat on low speed to mix.
5. Combine GEMS flour and baking soda and add to date mixture, beating lightly to blend.
6. Spoon into prepared muffin cups and bake 15 minutes.
7. Serve warm topped with Toffee Sauce (facing page).

TOFFEE SAUCE

⅓ cup brown sugar

2½ Tbsp soft butter

6 Tbsp whipping cream

1. Place brown sugar and butter in small saucepan and, stirring frequently, cook over medium-low heat for 3 minutes.
2. Pour cream slowly into sugar mixture and stir until sauce begins to bubble. Remove from heat. Serve warm.

YIELD: 6 servings

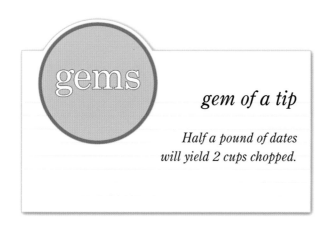

gems

gem of a tip

Half a pound of dates will yield 2 cups chopped.

BIBLIOGRAPHY

Anca, Alexandra. (2005). *Pocket Dictionary*. Mississauga, ON: Canadian Celiac Association.

Currie, V. & Spicer, K. (1993). *Full of Beans*. Campbellville, ON: Mighton House.

Drachman, L. and Wynne, P. (1990). *Great Grains*. New York, NY: Simon & Schuster.

Joachim, David. (2005). *The Food Substitutions Bible*. Toronto, ON: Robert Rose.

King Arthur Flour. (2003). *The King Arthur Flour Baker's Companion*. Woodstock, VT: Countryman Press.

Livingston, A.D. (2000). *The Whole Grain Cookbook*. New York, NY: Lyons Press.

Tessmer, K.A. (2003). *Gluten-Free for a Healthy Life*. New Jersey, NY: Career Press.

Williams, Chuck (Ed.). (2005). *Williams-Sonoma Baking*. Menlo Park, CA: Oxmoor House.

Wood, M. (1982). *Coping with the Gluten-Free Diet*. Springfield, IL: Charles C. Thomas.

Wood, R. (1999). *The Splendid Grain*. New York, NY: William Morrow.

gems

Your feedback is appreciated

Please send comments or inquiries to wendy@glutenfreegems.com or go to www.glutenfreegems.com

INDEX

CONVERSION CHARTS

The following conversions are approximate only, but the difference between the exact and the approximate conversion of various liquid and dry measures is minimal and will not affect cooking results.

The difference between one country's measuring cups and another's is within a 2 or 3 tsp variance.

TEMPERATURE

FAHRENHEIT	CENTIGRADE	GAS MARK	DESCRIPTION
150°F	65°C		
180°F	80°C		
200°F	95°C		
225°F	105°C	¼	Very cool
245°F	118°C		
250°F	120°C	½	
275°F	130°C	1	Cool
300°F	150°C	2	
325°F	165°C	3	Very moderate
350°F	180°C	4	Moderate
375°F	190°C	5	
400°F	200°C	6	Moderately hot
425°F	220°C	7	Hot
450°F	230°C	8	
475°F	245°C	9	Very hot

LENGTH

IMPERIAL	METRIC
⅛ inch	3 mm
¼ inch	6 mm
½ inch	12 mm
1 inch	2.5 cm
2 inches	5 cm
3 inches	8 cm
4 inches	10 cm
5 inches	12 cm
6 inches	15 cm
7 inches	18 cm
8 inches	20 cm
9 inches	23 cm
10 inches	25 cm
12 inches	30 cm

continues

VOLUME

LIQUID IMPERIAL	LIQUID OR DRY METRIC	LIQUID OR DRY CUPS/PINTS
1 fl oz	30 mL	⅛ cup
2 fl oz	60 mL	¼ cup
2½ fl oz	80 mL	⅓ cup
3 fl oz	100 ml	-
4 fl oz	125 mL	½ cup
5 fl oz	150 mL	¼ pint / 1 gill
-	160 mL	⅔ cup
6 fl oz	185 mL	¾ cup
8 fl oz	250 mL	1 cup
10 fl oz	300 mL	½ pint
12 fl oz	375 mL	1½ cups
14 oz (can)	398 mL	-
16 fl oz	500 mL	2 cups
20 fl oz	600 mL	2½ cups / 1 pint
24 fl oz	750 ml	3 cups
32 fl oz	1,000 mL / 1 litre	4 cups / 1¾ pints

WEIGHT

IMPERIAL	METRIC
1 oz	30 g
3 oz	90 g
6 oz	170 g
8 oz	225 g
10 oz	280 g
15 oz	425 g
1 lb	454 g
1½ lb	680 g
2 lb	900 g
3 lb	1.4 kg
4½ lb	2 kg
6½ lb	3 kg

LIQUID OR DRY TEASPOON / TABLESPOON
¼ tsp = 1.5 mL
½ tsp = 3 mL
1 tsp = 5 mL
3 tsp = 1 Tbsp or 15 mL
4 Tbsp = ¼ cup or 60 mL